Books by W.S. Merwin

From the Spanish Morning

From the Spanish Morning

Translations by

W.S. Merwin

With a Foreword by the Translator

Atheneum   1985   *New York*

On its original appearance *Spanish Ballads* was dedicated to Sylvia Plath and Ted Hughes, and the translation of *Lazarillo de Tormes* to Jane Kirstein.

Spanish Ballads: originally published in a clothbound edition by Abelard-Schuman (as *Some Spanish Ballads*) and as a paperback by Anchor Books (Doubleday) in 1961; copyright © 1961 by W.S. Merwin

Eufemia: originally published by the Tulane Drama Review in 1958; copyright © 1958 by W.S. Merwin

The Life of Lazarillo de Tormes: originally published by Anchor Books (Doubleday) in 1962; copyright © 1962 by W.S. Merwin

Library of Congress Cataloging in Publication Data
Main entry under title:

From the Spanish morning.

Bibliography: p.
Contents: Spanish ballads—Eufemia / Lope de Rueda
—The life of Lazarillo de Tormes.
1. Spanish literature—To 1500—Translations into
English. 2. Spanish literature—Classical period,
1500–1700—Translations into English. 3. English
literature—Translations from Spanish. I. Merwin,
W. S. (William Stanley), 1927–   . II. Some Spanish
ballads. 1984. III. Rueda, Lope de, d. 1565. Eufemia.
English. 1984. IV. Lazarillo de Tormes. English.
1984.
PQ6267.E1F7 1984   860'.8   84-70391
ISBN 0-689-11502-4 (pbk.)

Foreword: From the Spanish Morning

In the later hours of the day the morning is hard to recall. That first age of daylight, moving in its own time, cool, dewy, spacious, new, and already ancient like all beginnings—no sooner has it left than it seems improbable that it was ever there, that it happened once, that it was not only present but was the present and was everything. Trying to summon it again, to lay claim to it, we recognize how far from it we have come and how we have changed. We look at the surviving representations of it that were made, supposedly, from the life, when it was alive, and we find ourselves studying cracked carvings in stone, rags of tapestries, words in idioms no longer spoken and in conventions remote from ours. Between us and that fresh moment we encounter relics, fragments, shards of fact perpetuating distance, dust, and dust under it, and among all those we catch glimpses occasionally that appear to be revelations of ourselves, as we are now, in our only time.

The Spanish morning emerges, as mornings do, from the dark. The morning's words emerge from a night and a past that is no one's, and remind us of what we know but seem to have forgotten. In May 1910 Ramon Menendez Pidal, one of the pre-eminent Hispanic philologists of our age, and a lifelong student of the origins of the Spanish language and its earliest literature, read before the Real Academia Española a paper which he expanded, during the next decades, into a volume entitled, *The Spanish Language In Its First Ages*. In the completed work he asks whether it is possible "to make out, through the inadequate indications of the Arabic alphabet, those sounds which the Moors had heard spoken by the Romanic population of Spain which still lived among them." If that were possible, he said, "we would have some notion of the tongue that was spoken in the empire of the Visigoths on the day it fell."

v

With that hope in mind he quotes a legend of the Goths. At the time of their migration to Scythia, under their king Filimar—the story goes—a great bridge collapsed under the weight of the people and the animals they had with them, and many of them sank and were lost in the vast lakes and swamps which rendered that country impassable. To this day travellers through that region insist that they have heard, far in the distance, syllables and words of an unknown tongue, rising from the mouths drowned in the remote past.

The legend, in some form or other, must sound familiar to translators, and indeed to all readers, particularly of works from other languages and distant cultures. We are haunted by the sense that those voices are not wholly lost or altogether alien, and by the intimation that all utterances are telling our story and all beginnings have been our morning.

The works in this volume represent the beginnings of the literature of Spain, three aspects of it. In retrospect it seems at first that such an age must have been one of infinite possibility, which of course is true, in a sense, of any age, but is also an illusion produced by our own vantage-point. The range of possibilities never is, and never can be, entirely known to us. The possibilities themselves are always of our own making, and they must always appear to be offered, or at least in part determined, by the conditions and circumstances of an age that is just ending. There was a palimpsest of grammars and cultures on the Iberian peninsula long before any of these works existed. But the works themselves were conceived in a language which, for all the antiquity of its origins, was felt to be new.

One of the ironies of beginnings is that before long they seem archaic. They that are characteristically youthful become old. But the ballads—the *romances*—seem inseparable from the age of beginnings throughout the whole of their history, which in Spanish is remarkably long. (Indeed, if one includes some of the work of Machado, Hernandez, Lorca, even Neruda—and there is a good argument for doing so—it extends unbroken into our own time.) They seem to bring the beginning with them, the time of the legends and epics from which they evolved with the Spanish language itself, at the end of the Middle Ages. King Don Rodrigo, in the first *romances* in this collection, was the legendary last king of the Goths.

I have described something of the literary history of the *romances* in the introduction to the present selection, which is limited to the anonymous *romances* of the oral tradition. Many *romances* have been lost, but a rich canon has survived. I have placed this section first in the volume because its link with the buried voices is closest, most varied, and perhaps clearest. It is not the section which I translated first, though as it turns out it is the one I first hoped to translate. When I was nineteen, and obsessed with the craving to write poetry and to learn something about how to do it, I visited Ezra Pound in St. Elizabeth's Hospital, and he urged me to translate, as a way of learning something about the use of language. And what he suggested I work on was the *romancero*—the classical corpus of the oral Spanish ballads. I tried to take his advice at the time, and did indeed begin to make translations of a kind, but I could get nowhere with the *romancero* just then. Why he directed me to the *romances* I am not sure. He did not say, and I suppose awe, among other things, prevented me from asking until too late. I believe they were much in his mind in any case; he is known to have been intrigued by them for years. And from what I know of his own poetry, and from other pro-nouncements of his, and from the *romances* themselves as I came to know them better, I would guess that his reasons for com-mending them to me, if he had given any, would probably have included the fact, first of all, that the *romances* were not only in another language but were also at a safe remove in time and in culture, and so the dangers of imitation would be less insidious because real imitation would have been all but impossible. They were traditional, and so might entail some glimpse into the nature of tradition, which might be of value in our increasingly disjunct age. They were not—at least in their inception and in the age of their greatest flowering—literary, in the sense of being the written work of individuals concerned with fashions and careers. They combined great formality with great vigor, pure convention with great freedom, and they had the abiding freshness of common speech. I think there may have been still another reason for such a choice, having to do with the *romances'* continuing closeness to the origins of poetry. Months after our meeting and his first directives, Pound sent me—whether in response to some letter of mine or not I have forgotten now—a postcard on which he had scrawled in pencil, "Read seeds not twigs EP". His counsel is one of many things for which I am grateful to him, and the *romances* became, and remain for me, a miraculous source, trans-parent, constant, and inexhaustible.

In the years after Pound's suggestion I returned to them again and again and in time managed to make a few English versions of one or two, but it was more than a decade—during which I had done what I could to make a translation of *The Poem of the Cid*—before I felt that my representations of them in English conveyed anything at all of what I valued in the originals. They could not convey everything. They could not be the originals. They were translations, which are made by trying to do the impossible with what is possible. They were intended to indicate something, some life, that was there in the first language, rather than to be more or less familiar or fancy screens set up to obscure it.

Pound's brief suggestions, and a strong predisposition of my own, provided what little prompting I needed to believe that for me the practice of translation would be both a means of learning to attend to language and maybe to whatever gift for poetry I might have, and also a way of earning a livelihood—a spare one but one gained in my own time and in the exploration of my own persistent concerns. There was naivete—necessarily—in both convictions, and I am amazed at the unhesitating certainty with which I held them, and the luck that enabled me to put them to the test. Much of the luck was provided, in the early 1950's, by the BBC Third Programme, which commissioned me to translate works at my own suggestion from Spanish, French, and other languages, which were then performed on the radio. It was the BBC, for instance, that commissioned the translation of *The Poem of the Cid*, in 1952, and ran it in its entirety, as a serial, two years later. And they commissioned, soon afterwards, the Lope de Rueda translation of *Eufemia* that follows the *romances* in this volume.

I had suggested this play partly because of an interest, just then, in writing for the theater, perhaps in verse, but in any case in some mode that would not be confined to naturalism and yet could be spoken by contemporary actors, convincingly, without pointless mannerism or contortion. None of the few attempts at incorporating poetry into the theater that were around in the early 1950's sounded very promising to me. I had neither the advantages nor the habits of experience. And I was interested in the origins of drama itself as I was in the sources of poetry. The Elizabethan drama, which had been accepted as a more or less inevitable model for "poetic drama" for three and a half centuries seemed to me—much as I loved it—a dead hand for anyone who hoped to write for the theater in our age. At least its verse did. Its prose, the prose of Jonson and Shakespeare, Ford and Dekker and Middleton, was another matter, and an example that I thought might prove more useful. I was interested in the verse of the early

Hispanic theater, too, which was close to that of the *romances*, and in the prose which that theater developed as the secular drama evolved from its religious forbears. The proposal to translate Lope de Rueda's *Eufemia* was in fact part of a more ambitious plan to make translations of the rest of his principal plays, and of the lyrical plays of Gil Vicente, before him, which were descended directly from the religious plays of the end of the Middle Ages, and to go on to translate some of the later interlude plays of the Golden Age as well.

I have forgotten how it was that *Eufemia* was the play, out of that whole catalogue, that was chosen first. It is arranged first among Lope de Rueda's collected comedies, and I may have been simply starting at the beginning. It presents a particular curiosity to readers of English, since it is based on the same tale of Boccaccio's from which Shakespeare took the plot for *Cymbeline*.

As for Lope de Rueda himself, he is identified usually as one of the precursors of the great age of Spanish drama, the age of Calderon and of the more famous Lope, Lope de Vega. Sometimes the descriptions seem to imply that Lope de Rueda was a somewhat crude, unfinished writer, interesting chiefly to literary history, which seems to me quite unjust. He is complete as he is, and the vitality of his language and of his characters is still there for anyone who will take the trouble to listen, but—like the prose of Jonson and Ford—it is muffled in a convention that is strange to us, and requires of us a particular effort. Lope's place in the development of the Spanish theater made him especially interesting to me, perhaps for the same reasons that EP had written what he had on the postcard. The seeds seemed to me to contain the whole story.

Lope de Rueda's comedies, and his prose, were secular, as Boccaccio was secular, and like Boccaccio—the man and the work—they were not yet far from the shadow of the church. The rhetoric and burlesque of his comic characters, and their actions, have one of their roots in the mock sermons, clowned by impersonators dressed up as church dignitaries, which were delivered—until they were forbidden there—in the churches themselves, on the Day of the Holy Innocents. They seem to have another root in a source that may be older than the church itself: the current of folk humor that produced Punch and Judy and the clowns of Aristophanes. In the first decades of the 16th century there was a wave of adaptations and imitations of Greek and Latin plays in Spanish, written for the most part by humanists, to be read by other humanists rather than to be performed. The interest in the secular classics was involved with the new influence of Italy on Spanish culture. The Spanish conquests in Italy were followed by waves of Spanish travellers and emigrants from all classes and callings, some of whom settled there permanently. By the second quarter of the 16th century, wandering troupes of Italian actors, performing Italian comedies, were familiar visitors in the cities and towns of Spain, and Lope de Rueda, an actor himself, found in Italian comedy suggestions for his own mature work.

His first biographer, and an impassioned admirer, was Cervantes, born almost half a century after he was. Cervantes tells us that Lope de Rueda was "a native of Seville, and born to the trade of gold-beater or goldsmith. He had a great gift for pastoral poetry and in that mode no one surpassed him then or since. And though I was a boy at the time and so was not a sure judge of the merit of his verses, those that remain in my memory now in my later years confirm what I have just said." Cervantes says of the theater of Lope's youth, "At the time . . . all the trappings of a writer of comedies were kept in a sack, and amounted to four white shepherd's jackets decorated with tooled and gilded leather, four beards and wigs, and four shepherd's crooks, more or less. The comedies consisted of conversations like eclogues, involving two or three shepherds and some shepherdess or other. They were dolled up and drawn out with two or three interludes, sometimes a negress, sometimes a ruffian, or a fool, or a foreigner . . ." and this was the sort of theatrical convention which Lope de Rueda had to work with.

Nothing is known, except by inference, of his schooling, and nothing of how his talents were first revealed and how he came to follow them. Perhaps what he followed first, leaving his gold-beating, was a troupe of travelling actors. He embraced that life at some point, and it was a calling that had a bad name in the established society of that age, as rovers tend to have in any time. Yet Lope shone in the profession and by the middle of the century was being commissioned to provide entertainments, religious and secular, for court festivities—entertainments which he directed and perhaps wrote himself.

He was married, by then, to a remarkable and original woman, an actress named Mariana who, before her marriage, had been a member of the household of Don Gaston de la Cerda, the third Duke of Medinaceli. Her story came to light early in this century, through the researches of Narciso Alonso A. Cortes into a lawsuit brought by Lope de Rueda against the Duke, and was recounted by Emilio Cotarelo in the Real Academia edition of Lope's work, in 1908.

Don Gaston, his parents' second son, was born in 1504, and so was roughly of an age with Lope de Rueda. He was frail as a child, sickly and lame. The family marked him for the church, and he became a monk in the monastery of San Bartolomé de Lupiana. But his elder brother died without an heir and Don Gaston set about trying to extricate himself from holy orders, going so far as to obtain a papal dispensation to permit him to resume secular status. And he urged his father to make him heir to the title. Don Gaston's younger brother, Don Juan, objected, and so did their mother. The old Duke persuaded them all to accept a compromise: Don Gaston would have the inheritance for his own lifetime but would not be allowed to marry, and after his death the title and holdings would pass to his brother's line.

In 1544 the old Duke died, and Don Gaston entered upon his inheritance. He joined the Order of the Knights of Malta, with the title of Grand Prior of Castile. And he turned over most of the actual property to his brother, who before long came to act as the Duke, while Don Gaston withdrew to Cogolludo and lived in retirement as a semi-invalid with a fondness for undemanding amusements.

The following year two women on their way to Aragon stopped at the Duke's house. They sang and they danced, and the Duke heard them and saw them and was so enchanted by Mariana in particular that he asked her to remain in his household. Her companion continued the journey without her. Mariana's musical gifts were a marvel to her contemporaries, who spoke of her talents in hyperboles. The Duke became so addicted to her company, as well as to her singing and dancing, that he had her hair cut and dressed her as a page, in breeches, taking her with him hunting and wherever else he went, and indulging a quite obvious pleasure in seeing her dressed as a man. He promised to pay her handsomely for her attendance, and even to provide her with a good dowry and a husband, but he died without having done either, when she had been in his service for six years. Soon after his death she married Lope de Rueda, who brought suit, subsequently, against the new heir, for his wife's unpaid salary, and won. Not the whole of the demand, but a considerable part of it.

As far as can be determined from the scattered references to Lope de Rueda and to performances of comedies and pageants for which he was responsible in one capacity or another, he travelled from city to city in Spain for some years, part of the time no doubt with his own company, and spent long periods in Madrid and Valencia. More than once he is known to have provided theatrical performances for court personages. He died in Cordoba in 1565, or so it is supposed from the date of his will, made in the house of Diego Lopez, schoolmaster, in March of that year, while Lope was "sound of will" but already too sick to sign it. He asked to be buried in the great church of Cordoba, beside his daughter Juana, and according to Cervantes his remains were laid there between the two choir stalls. His will itemizes articles of clothing, braziers, copper utensils, locked away in chests that he had left behind in the far-off city of Toledo, in the house of an inn-keeper, and linens stored in that city in the wardrobes of a shoemaker: "six sheets of ordinary linen, and another with lace borders, two lace pillows, a lace fruit-cover, three tablecloths with velvet edges . . ." It is a glimpse of daily domestic details that he himself would not see again, possessions already beyond his reach. His wife Mariana had died some years before, and he had re-married. "I declare that I left in that same city of Toledo, in pawn to a jeweler known to Angela Rafaela, my lawful wife, a silver belt worth two ducats. . . . It is my will that it be redeemed." ". . . in pawn in the house of the linen-merchant Herrera, in the above-named city, a bed . . . worth eight ducats . . . to be re-deemed." It is also a catalogue, not only of things that had be-longed to him but of his debts and his residences and perennial financial troubles in Toledo and in Seville (and we know of an-other encounter with creditors in Madrid, four years before his death)—a survey of an existence that must have been restless and daring and precarious.

A few years after his death his writings were edited and pub-lished in several collections by his friend Juan de Timoneda: the four prose comedies, the one in verse; three pastoral colloquies, and a series of comic *pasos*: sketches which could be performed independently, or set between scenes of other plays as interludes, without altering the main story; a "Deaf Man Farce" (of doubtful ascription), a "Dialogue on Breeches" etc. Just the same, some of his writings were lost, and some, including a youthful satire on doctors, a forerunner of Moliere's, were re-discovered and pub-lished within the last century.

The prose comedies form the main body of the work, and there is no sure way of dating them or knowing the order in which the plays were written. *Eufemia* seems to be a typical mature piece, an example of the conventions which Lope inherited and helped to transform: the broad farce and the high-flown romantic rhetoric, the Italian main plot turning upon deceptions contrived and discovered, and the burlesque interludes. It is not, and does not pretend to be, a drama of subtle psychological delineation or of piercing cosmic insight. Its virtues, like those of the Italian comedy which was its foster parent, are those that we have come to describe as "operatic," and of course their kinship with Italian opera is obvious. They are virtues not of analysis but of presentation and effect. They assume a considerable familiarity with the theatrical conventions, the characters, and often with elements of the particular story. They rely upon the rolling rhetorical texture of the language and the satisfaction of certain clearly indicated expectations for the empathy on which they depend. The characterization is broad, and the personae are easily recognized stock figures. The convention altogether, light as it is, and with no pretense of naturalism, is akin to what Harley Granville-Barker, speaking of the mock trial on the moor in *King Lear*, calls "pure drama." It is something that "cannot be rendered into other terms than its own. . . . The sound of the dialogue matters almost more than the meaning. . . ." And yet the language and action are closer to Jonson or Ford or Dekker than to Shakespeare; most of Shakespeare. The plots, characters, and the flourishes of rhetoric are no longer familiar to us, so we have no ready expectations in approaching a comedy such as *Eufemia*. We do not have an acting tradition, either, that might render the speeches with confidence and ease, and any performance at all of such a play, in our time, would be a rarefied curiosity. But *Eufemia*, like the rest of Lope's comedies, was written to entertain as a performance. Reading it, in another age, in another country, in another language, is a little like hearing the ballads, Spanish or Scottish, without their music. Something is missing and we are not ever sure what it is. But something of their life makes us go on listening to what we think they are. And *Eufemia* is alive—or I think it is. It must be read, if possible, as though it were being performed. But then some of its life, if I am right about it, must be ours in any case.

As a matter of literary history, Lope de Rueda's relation to the great playwrights of the Spanish Golden Age, who followed him, Guillén de Castro, Lope de Vega, Calderon de la Barca, bears some resemblance to the place of *Lazarillo de Tormes* in relation to the work of Cervantes. At once whole in itself, and a herald of larger things to come. Editions of *Lazarillo* were circulating more than ten years before Lope de Rueda's death. Three editions, in three different cities, Burgos, Alcalá de Henares, and Antwerp, were published in 1554, and there are grounds for supposing that another edition, ancestor of all of them, had been published in Antwerp in 1553, though no copy has been found in modern times. The book was published anonymously, and it has even been suggested that Lope de Rueda may have written it. But it is one ascription among several, and is considered unlikely. The author was certainly not—though that naive suggestion has been made too—the shrewd, pragmatic, likeable hero of the story, except in the same way that Huckleberry Finn was Mark Twain.

The book was immediately and spectacularly successful with all classes that could read, and its popularity was so general, five years after its publication, that the Inquisition placed it on the Index, probably because of its satirical portraits of the priest and the pedlar of indulgences. But copies continued to be smuggled in from abroad, and Philip II, fifteen years later, had a bowdlerized edition published in Spain which was kept in print for another three decades at least. Speculation about its authorship has exercised scholars for three and a half centuries, and the definition of the *genre*, the "picaresque novel," which *Lazarillo* and its imitators fostered, has preoccupied literary historians and critics for over a century. An "anti-hero," of low birth with no trace of "honor" to it, which must have been particularly striking in a society in which the fantasies of all classes and callings had been fattened on the overblown fare of the last romances of chivalry, and in which the fevered excitability surrounding the word and concept of "honor" provided, or was evoked to provide, a justification for most human activities. The figure usually tells his (or her) own story, which is episodic, "horizontal," and concerned for the most part with ordinary survival, in a series of situations that include working in a menial capacity for a succession of masters who are described in a manner which critics have agreed to call "realism": it is direct, rapid, flat-footed, and often funny, and it conjures up characters, scenes, and situations from daily life which must have been instantly and astonishingly familiar to every reader. It is often said that the language is unadorned, but in *Lazarillo* the subtleties of irony, including the occasional, casual classical references, and the sureness of tone, provide an elegance and an authority, a style, which is far from ordinary, and which any further ornament would spoil.

The irony and its elegance, its scope and sadness and humor, reappear, employed on a far vaster scale and playing over a richer variety of circumstances and emotions, in the great prose of Cervantes, early in the following century. Of course he knew *Lazarillo* intimately; some of the most assured, brilliant, and haunting writing in his *Novelas Ejemplares*, written in the first decade of the seventeenth century and published in 1613, is cast in what by then had become the picaresque mode. There is, above all, the story of *Rinconete and Cortadillo*, two urchins of Seville, agile in body and in wit. One can see elements of Lazarillo's history transformed again, still later, in *Don Quijote*: the fully elaborated contrast between the late fooleries of chivalric idealism and the hard edges of the everyday world projected into two distinct characters. The episodic structure and the curiously refracted views of situation after situation. There is a whole literature exploring the influence of *Lazarillo* on Cervantes.

Elements of that convention—the anti-hero, the attempt at a "realistic" presentation, the episodic structure, even some of the irony—had occurred in literature for a long time: in Apuleius; in the stories of Sinbad; even, as we have come to see in fictions far more remote: the recurring trickster, the escaper, the survivor, the perennial exception who is the real rule. But *Lazarillo* is a remarkably transparent crystallization, and either directly or via Cervantes he has had an influence on writers and books long since his story was first told, some of whom may never have heard of him. He was first translated into English by David Rouland in 1576, and was variously imitated in Elizabethan England, where the book would obviously have found sympathetic readers—most notably in Nashe's *The Unfortunate Traveller*. *Lazarillo*, the book and protagonist, and no doubt many of their imitators, appear to have suggested to Grimmelshausen some of the outlines of his anti-hero "Simplicissimus," late in the 17th century. Defoe, and then Fielding, and in France Lesage with his *Gil Blas de Santillane*, were the debtors, and sometimes the successors, of the unknown author. At a still greater distance, it seems likely that Gogol's *Dead Souls* would not have been the same book, at least without *Lazarillo* and his influence on Cervantes. And in our own age, however the protagonists may have been conceived, the same could be said of Collodi's *Pinocchio* and of *Huckleberry Finn*.

But *Lazarillo*'s interest, the life of the book and of its central character, are no more limited to literary history than Mark Twain's, or Gogol's, or Grimmelshausen's books and their heroes. For all his imitators, *Lazarillo* is unique, and indefinably pure, and so is his account of who he is and of the world that he has survived. *Lazarillo de Tormes* has been translated into English a number of times since Rouland's version, and when the suggestion to make a new English translation arose in a conversation with Carl Morse, who was then an editor at Doubleday, with whom I was working on the Anchor edition of *Spanish Ballads*, I considered for a while just what I might hope to gain in trying once more. I decided to do it, I suppose, for the same reasons that often operate in such circumstances: something in the original that I hoped to present a bit more closely than it had been presented before, something that would be closer to particular characteristics of the original that I valued. The character himself, of course, but the character as he is conveyed by the language, with all its shadings of irony, its light touch, its directness and apparent simplicity. Yet neither the hero nor the author nor their style were really simple at all, and the text, their text, was comic besides, which presents any translator with impossibilities of its own. If I were to put forward in English a Lazarillo who was correct but dull I would have misrepresented him and what he says altogether. Of the three sections in this volume, *Lazarillo* is the one that was translated last, and in some respects it was the most difficult, partly because it had to seem, word by word, so plain. *Lazarillo*, after all, really is an original, and I hoped, as others had, to hear him alive, in English.

April 1984, Maui

Contents

Spanish Ballads

Introduction

The ballads of Spain are called *romances*. The word "ballad" is not an ideal translation of the Spanish name for these poems and is pressed into service, for want of a better, in the interests of simplicity. For one thing, calling them "ballads" gives a misleading notion of the form of the Spanish poems. It inevitably arouses an anticipation of the familiar ballad meters of the Scottish and English popular traditions. The forms of the Spanish *romances* are quite different—they look different on the page and they sound different (in general, although there are some cases where the Spanish poems and those of the northern popular traditions seem to echo each other's cadences as well as bits of each other's stories). Besides, it is only very roughly true to say that these poems are to the Spanish tradition what the ballads are to the traditions of Scotland and England. No popular poetic tradition in these countries compares to the place of the *romances* in the culture of Spain. This is not just because the sheer bulk of the Spanish *romance* literature exceeds that of the ballads of the British Isles. The *romances*, Spaniards and students of Spain have agreed, are one of the essential keys to Spain—not only the Spain of the late Middle Ages, but that of the twentieth century.

In the purely literary history of Spain the *romances* occupy a unique position. They grew so naturally out of the decay of the Spanish popular epic poetry that it is hard to say whether some of the oldest *romances* are separate poems out of more or less complete cycles, or fragments of lost epics. For several centuries, throughout all of Spain and the Spanish-speaking world the *romances* were a kind of universal poetry, not only remembered, repeated, and loved, but also composed by unlearned and by literate poets alike. They exerted an important influence on the rest of Spanish poetry: many of the lyric forms of the great age of Spanish literature show their *romance* parentage very plainly. The process worked the other way around too, and the *romance* tradition absorbed and reshaped a number of popular lyric forms as they fell into decadence. In the development of the Spanish drama the *romance* tradition was crucial. Some of the playwrights of the Golden Age simply dramatized events and stories which has already been shaped, developed, and sometimes in great part invented, over the course of several hundred years, by the thousands of imaginations through which the *romances* had passed. And the chief verse form of the Spanish classical drama—light, rapid, flexible, capable of great elegance or of colloquial abruptness without apparent strain—again bears a marked family resemblance to the main verse form of the *romances*. As for Spanish prose literature, there is no need to persuade anyone who has read *Don Quixote* that the *romances* were real and present to Cervantes, as they were to other novelists of his time. Both the music and the content of the *romances* pervade much of the imaginative literature of the great ages of Spain. The Spanish Golden Age and the last age of the *romances* ended virtually together.

But if they ended as literature the *romances* began as something else. From some indeterminate period before the twelfth century until late in the fifteenth the Iberian peninsula (and France and other parts of Europe) supported wandering performers who were responsible for the rise of one of the main poetic traditions in several of the countries where they flourished. The Spanish name for these professional performers was *juglares*, a word which (like the French *jongleur* and ultimately the English "juggler") comes from the Latin word *ioculari*—jokes—or *ioculator*—someone who entertains a crowd or a king by making them laugh: a joker, a clown. How the *juglares* themselves came into being is no longer known, but the generally accepted theory is that they derived from the wandering street entertainers of Rome and that their development was influenced by the bards and minstrels of the barbarian peoples. They are known to have existed in Spain by the seventh century, but it is not until the twelfth that they emerge into history as surveyors and fabricators of epic poetry.

In its heyday the word *juglar* was used more or less indiscriminately to describe people as different as the *trovadores* or literate poets (who eventually, in several of the Romance languages, but most notably in Provençal, evolved a lyric tradition of great freshness, originality and beauty) and the clowns who went around with performing monkeys. Not everyone remained happy about this easygoing nomenclature. The *trovadores* came to consider themselves not only superior to the rest of the *juglares* but separate from them; they made it clear that they *composed* but did not *perform* their verses. Their lot as a class rose until some of them became very rich, although their individual fortunes were not always so comfortable and some of the *trovadores* sank to the position of wandering minstrels, which was what the *juglares*, properly speaking, were. The *juglares* (in this more precise sense of the word) sang and recited the epic *cantares*; they might be accompanied in their performances by mimes, known as *remendadores*, and *cazurros*—a name which included clowns and most varieties of stunt men.

The *trovadores*, socially and politically, were drawn in two directions—on the one hand toward becoming court poets and developing a special poetry to fit courtly circumstances, and on the other toward the popular tradition and the supplying of narrative verse to the *juglares*, who would pay for it in order, themselves, to make a living with it. The second of these two impulses was the older, and it is the one which concerns the origins of the *romances*.

For their sources the *trovadores* relied upon such material as Carolingian history and legends, or the history and legends of Spain—the life and triumphs of the Cid, for example, or of Fernán-González, or the tragic stories of King Don Rodrigo, "the last of the Goths," or Bernardo del Carpio, or the Seven Princes of Lara—or the stories of classical antiquity or the Bible. There is no doubt that there were complete *cantares*, as full and finished as *El Cantar del Mio Cid*, dealing with these and many other subjects, but none of them has survived except in fragments or in prose transcripts in later chronicles.

The verse in which the epic *cantares* was composed looks like this when written down (the passage is from *The Poem of the Cid*):

De los sos ojos   tan fuertemientre llorando,
tornava la cabeca   i estávalos catando.
Vió puertas abiertas   e ucos sin canados,
alcándaras vazias   sin pieles e sin mantos
e sin falcones   e sin adtores mudados.

(From his eyes   bitterly weeping,
He turned his head   and stayed looking back at them.
He saw doors standing open   and gates without fastenings.
The racks empty   without furs and without mantles
And without falcons   and without mewed goshawks.)

Scholars have spent much time and argument in trying to establish the rules upon which this kind of verse was written and what its sources are, and at last have virtually agreed that it was for the most part, at least, an indigenous Spanish form, and that there was no rigid metrical or syllabic pattern to which the poets were trying to conform. Rather, the verse, mechanically speaking, was a relatively free form which the *trovadores* played by ear and adapted to the needs of their narrative. Still, it is possible to make a few generalizations. The epic *cantares* were composed in a long flexible line with a marked break somewhere in the middle. The nearest equivalent in the English tradition is the Middle English line in which *Piers Plowman* is written. However, the Spanish line does not have the regular accentual pattern of the Middle English verse, nor its alliterative scheme. At least in historical theory it tends to a normal length of sixteen syllables. The lines end not in rhyme but in an assonance pattern. In the passage quoted above the last two syllables of each line are the vowels *a-o:* llor*a*nd*o*, cat*a*nd*o*, can*a*d*o*s, etc. An assonance pattern of this kind can run on for a hundred lines or more, or may change after five or six.

The latter part of the fourteenth century saw the decline of the epic tradition in Spain. Not only did the sources themselves dry up, from causes and at a time which are both largely unknown to history, but the existing poems were sung less and less often, and gradually, since they had not been written down, were lost. But not entirely. Isolated episodes, situations, descriptions, characters, refrains would be remembered, repeated and sung, in private, for the pleasure of it. They would retain the sound and the formal elements of the lost epics. Gradually they began to take on a shape and completeness of their own, and the *romances* were born.

They can be (and occasionally, for reasons of space, they are) printed to look like the verse of the epic *cantares;* but it is more usual to treat the halves of the old line as two separate lines, so that a passage of a *romance* usually looks like this:

> *Ya se partia el buen Cid*
> *sin al rey besar la mano;*
> *ya se parte de sus tierras,*
> *de Vivar y sus palacios:*
> *las puertas deja cerradas,*
> *los alamudes echados,*
> *las cadenas deja llenas*
> *de podencos y de galgos;*

solo lleva sus falcones,
los pollos y los mudados.

(Now the good Cid has gone
Without kissing the King's hand;
Now he goes from his lands,
From Vivar and its palaces:
He leaves the doors closed
And the bolts fastened,
He leaves on their chains
The hounds and the grayhounds,
He takes only his falcons,
The fledglings and the mewed birds.)

This passage and the one from *The Poem of the Cid* describe the same departure. The differences in the two narratives are obvious, but the two passages, at different stages of the same tradition, are, formally, virtually the same. The *romance*, however, is more regular; the lines keep closer to their norm of eight syllables each, and the rhythm is more regular than in the older poem. The assonance pattern remains (m*a*no, pal*a*cio, ech*a*dos, etc.), and the over-all rhythm of the poetry still runs in units of two lines, every two lines corresponding to one line in the old *cantares*. As the *romances* moved further and further away from their epic origins the pause at the end of the second line sometimes grew fainter. In some of the literary *romances* of the seventeenth century the assonances are virtually all that is left to recall this element of the old rhythmic scheme. However, the pause pattern was never lost in the popular literature, and is still unmistakably there in traditional *romances* collected in Spain and South America in this century. This unbroken connection with the indigenous popular epics of the Middle Ages is one thing which makes the Spanish *romances* unique among the ballad literatures of the rest of Europe.

As might have been expected, in the period of the decay of the *cantares* the parts of the epics which were usually remembered were those in which a single situation stood out in intense relief against a background of historical or legendary narrative. In the *romances* the purely narrative elements were gradually reduced, simplified, or merely lost, and more and more emphasis came to be placed on the lyrical development of a situation.

One of the distinct characteristics of the Spanish *cantares*, in comparison with the French *chansons de geste* and other popular epics of the Middle Ages, had been a capacity for dealing with contemporary, or nearly contemporary, experience. *The Poem of*

The Cid was written only forty-some years after the death of its hero, and from what evidence remains it seems likely that some of the other Spanish epics dealt with historical events which were no further removed from the period in which they were first sung. The *romances* carried on this tradition. Until the *genre* degenerated into a merely literary imitation of its former self there were *romances* which narrated the battles, memorable events, the lives and deaths of the great figures of their own times. Of course ballads of this kind are common in other literatures too, but Spain is particularly rich in this kind of historical poetry.

Early in their development, Spanish *romances* came to include the simple, single-episode stories which one immediately thinks of when ballads are mentioned. Some of these stories—the identical situations—can be found in many of the ballad literatures of Europe. There is, for instance, the universally popular story of the adulterous wife whose vengeful husband visits her in the guise of her lover, in *The Mistress of Bernal Francés*. This poem is a good example, too, of the economy and dramatic precision which abound in the *romances*. The richness of descriptive detail heightens the suspense in a situation whose outcome, as the reader is made to feel at the beginning, cannot fail to be tragic; and the echo of these descriptions in the husband's quiet and deadly promises to his wife adds to the feeling of terror at the end of the poem. This *romance* illustrates another characteristic of these Spanish poems: in comparison with most other ballad literatures, the *romances* are deliberately abrupt and apparently fragmentary. It became virtually a convention to develop a situation until its consequences were just visible and then stop short rather than describe them. One theory suggests that the taste for this kind of conclusion was a result of the genuinely fragmentary nature of the early *romances*. But it is also true that this love of concision and implication rather than elaboration runs through much of Spanish popular poetry; it can be found, for instance, in the very short, compressed forms of the popular lyric—the *copla*, the *estribillo*, etc.—in which, again, Spanish poetry is enormously rich.

The seven hundred years' war with the Moors was one of the chief formative experiences in the history and culture of Spain. One of its more obvious effects upon Spanish literature was the creation of a kind of *romance* which narrates the experience of war, love, captivity, or whatever it may be, from a Moorish, or at least a fictitiously Moorish, point of view. There are several of these *romances* in this selection.

The Jewish population of Spain, on the other hand, developed a rich, intense poetry in its own Spanish-Jewish dialect, including a body of *romances*; some of these are included also. Not only Castilian but all of the Romance languages of the Iberian peninsula—Catalán, Aragonés, Galician, Portuguese, to name the main ones—can boast large numbers of *romances* even today, many of them variants of well-known poems which exist in Castilian, but some of them to be found nowhere else. "The Corpse-Keeper" and "One Castle, Two Castles" are from Catalán, not Castilian, originals.

During the sixteenth and seventeenth centuries the *romance* underwent several changes. *Romances* were composed unselfconsciously by cultivated poets who wrote in other forms as well. They were used for satire, for verse epistles, for epigrams and epitaphs which assumed no narrative context at all. Some of the new *romances* gave utterance to the amorous elegiac laments of the same shepherds and shepherdesses who are to be found elsewhere in the Renaissance literature of Europe. These *romances* are, too, more lyric and meditative, less narrative or dramatic than the older, traditional ones. I have included poems which illustrate these latter developments of the form, and also an example of those (relatively late) *romances* which vouched for the veracity of marvels and prodigies—as did Autolycus's piece about

"... *a fish that appeared upon the coast on Wednesday the fourscore of April, forty thousand fathom above water, and sung this ballad against the hard hearts of maids. It was thought she was a woman* ..."

and such English wonder-mongering ballads as the one (which, most wonderful of all, was true) about the Genoese Siamese Twins, John Baptist and Lazarus Colloretti, of whom it was established at the start that

"... *a Gentleman well qualifide*
Doth bear his brother at his side
Inseparably knit."

All of the pieces in this selection are anonymous, which makes dating them, and consequently any kind of chronological arrangement, very difficult. The date when a poem was first written down of course tells nothing about the date of its origin, and scholarship has to rely on internal evidence to determine the age of many *romances*. I have arranged the poems in groups starting with the early legendary and historical cycles and ending with the marvel-mongering piece: this method of presenting them is in fact very roughly chronological, but its only real virtue is convenience.

It would be far from correct to call the language of the *romances* "natural," since it is the result of a highly developed poetic convention and of loving artifice, but it is simple, direct, precise. At its best it seems both inevitable and unexpected. The rhythm of the poems is sinewy, spare, and fluent. These qualities, and the literal sense of the poems, are what I have tried to evoke in English. In some *romances*, particularly in the earlier ones which evolved directly from the *cantares*, the use of the present and past tenses differs considerably from that of modern English—or modern Spanish, for that matter. It has been suggested that, at least in the epics themselves, the present tense was used to bring a scene or a detail into the foreground, and the past tenses to give the effect of distance whether in time or space. In translating the poems I have for the most part preferred to alter the tenses as little as possible unless they sounded hopelessly awkward or confusing in English. It seemed to me that in retaining, as a general rule, the same use of tenses as the originals, the translations were brought a shade closer to the Spanish poems. On the other hand, I have made no attempt to match the assonance patterns of the originals with English rhymes. Rhyme does not come as naturally to English as assonances do to Spanish—especially in cases where sets of thirty or forty rhymes on one sound might be called for. Some approximation to the assonances of the originals would of course have been possible, but it would inevitably have involved distortion of language and a certain clogging of the rhythm. My aim was not to produce a series of virtuoso performances but a group of translations which would be faithful and readable, and would get in the way of the originals as little as possible.

I wish to express my gratitude to Mr. P. Harvey of Queen Mary College, University of London, for helping me with some of the problems of translation, and to the Hispanic Council and its librarians for their patient generosity.

W. S. MERWIN

London
January 1960

Contents

3. *Historical* Romances

4. *Moorish* Romances *and* Romances *of Captives*

5. *Late Lyric* Romances

Contents

6. *A Wonder-Mongering* Romance

1. Romances *from the epic cycles*

La Cava Florinda's Fatal Immodesty

With gaiety and delight
La Cava and her maidens
Went out from a tower of the palace
By a postern gate
And made their way to a garden
Close to a dense grove
Of jasmins and myrtle trees
Grown in tangles and thickets.
Beside a fountain which spilled
Crystal and echoing pearls
From six spouts of fine gold
Among bulrushes and lilies,
The maidens took their ease
Seeking comfort and relief
From the fire of their youth
And the heat of summer.
They gave their arms to the water,
And, by its coldness tempted,
La Cava was the first
Who cast off her clothes.
In the shadowy pool
So fair her body shone
That, like the sun,
She eclipsed all others there.
She thought that she and her maidens
Were alone, but as it happened,
Through the dense ivy
King Rodrigo was watching.
And that moment kindled
Fire in his proud heart,
And love, with beating wings,
Inflamed him without warning.
This was the luckless beginning
Which brought on the loss of Spain:
An unlucky woman
And a man given up to love.
Florinda lost her flower,

The King suffered his punishment;
She said he forced her to it,
He said she gave full consent.
As for which of those two
Was more blameworthy,
Men will tell you it was La Cava,
And women, Rodrigo.

The Dream of King Don Rodrigo

The winds were roused,
The moon was at full,
The fishes made wailing cries
At the wild weather
While the good King Don Rodrigo
Slept beside La Cava
In a sumptuous tent
Adorned with gold all over.
Three hundred ropes of silver
Were what held it there,
Within were a hundred maidens
In wonderful apparel,
Fifty playing instruments
With marvelous accord,
Fifty of them singing
To a sweet air.
Then spoke a maiden,
Fortune was her name:
—King Don Rodrigo,
If you sleep, wake, I pray you,
And you will see your sad fate
And your worse ending,
And behold your people dead
And your army routed
And your towns and cities
In one day destroyed,
Your castles, fortresses,
Ruled by another lord.
Ask me who has done this,
I will tell you plainly:
Count Don Julián,
Out of love for his daughter
Because you dishonored her
And she was all he had;
He has sworn an oath
Which will cost you your life.—
He awoke in great anguish
At the sound of that voice;

With sad and woeful face
Thus he replied:
—Fortune, for your message
I am grateful to you.—
At that moment there arrived
One who brought tidings
That the Count Don Julián
Was laying waste the lands.
He calls at once for his horse
And rides forth to meet him;
So many are his foes
That his courage avails nothing;
His captains and soldiers flee,
Each one as he can.

The Defeat of King Don Rodrigo

The hosts of Don Rodrigo
Took panic and fled.
In the eighth battle
His enemies conquered.
Rodrigo leaves his tents
And goes from the kingdom,
Alone in his wretchedness
He rides with no company,
His horse for weariness
Can scarcely go forward,
It wanders at its will;
He does nothing to guide it.
So faint is the King
That his senses are numb,
Dead with thirst and hunger,
Woeful to behold;
So red with blood,
He looks like a live coal.
His weapons are hacked,
That were crusted with jewels,
His sword like a saw-blade
With the blows it had taken,
His helmet so battered
It had sunk down on his head,
His face swollen
With the ordeal he had suffered.
    He comes to the top of a hill,
The highest one in sight,
From there he beholds his people
Fleeing in defeat,
From there he sees his banners
And the standards that once were his
Trampled into the earth
Till the ground covers them,
He looks for his captains
But none is to be seen,
He sees the field red with blood
Running off in rivers.

The wretched man, at the sight,
Is overcome with grief,
And weeping from his eyes
In this manner he speaks:
—Yesterday I was King of Spain,
Today not of one village;
Yesterday I had towns and castles,
Today I have not one;
Yesterday I had servants
And people to wait upon me;
Today there is not a battlement
Which I can call my own.
Ill-fated was the hour
And the day luckless
When I was born and fell heir
To so great an heritage
Since I was to lose it
In one day, all together!
Why do you not come, Death,
And take this soul of mine
From this wretched body
Which would be grateful to you?

The Penance of King Don Rodrigo

    King Don Rodrigo
When he had lost Spain
Departed in despair,
Fleeing from his ill fortune;
The luckless man went alone,
Wanting no company,
But the pain of Death
Followed close behind him.
He took his way to the mountains
Where they looked most forbidding.
He happened upon a shepherd
Who was herding his flock;
He said to him— Good man,
Answer me this:
Are there churchmen nearby,
Or is there a monastery?—
Then the shepherd answered
That none such would he find
For in all that wilderness
There was no one but a hermit
In a hermitage
Living a holy life.
When he heard this the King was happy
To think he might end his life there;
He asked the shepherd to give him
Food, if he had any,
For the strength of his body
Was deserting him utterly.
The shepherd brought out a bag
Where he kept his bread,
He gave some to the King, and some salt beef
Which he happened to have there.
It was very black, that bread;
The King found it bitter;
Tears rose into his eyes,
He could not check them,
When he thought of all the things
That he had tasted in his lifetime.

20

When he had rested he asked
The way to the hermitage;
The shepherd showed it to him,
So that he should not be lost.
The King gave him a chain
And a ring which he had with him,
Jewels of great price
Which the King had treasured.
He set out on his way.
As the sun was sinking
He came to the hermitage
At the top of the mountains.
He found the hermit,
Who was more than a hundred years old.
—I am the wretched Rodrigo
Who at one time was king,
Who, by love led astray,
Has forfeited his soul,
And for whose black sins
All Spain lies in ruins.
In God's name, hermit, I beg you,
And in the name of Santa María,
To hear my confession,
For I wish for my life to end.—
The hermit was filled with alarm
And answered him, in tears:
—I will hear your confession,
But I cannot absolve you.—
When he had spoken these words
They heard a voice from heaven:
—Absolve him, confessor,
Upon your life absolve him,
And in his own tomb
Give him a penance.—
As it was revealed to him,
The King carried it out:
He laid himself in the tomb
By the side of the hermitage;
In it there slept a serpent,
It was horrible to behold;
Three times round the tomb it was coiled;
It had seven heads.
—Offer prayers for me, hermit,

That I may end my life well.—
The hermit spoke words of courage,
Then covered him with the tombstone.
Beside it, he prayed to God
All the hours of the day.
—Penitent, how fares it with you,
With your strong companion—
—Now he is gnawing me, gnawing me
Where I most sinned,
He is gnawing straight into my heart,
The fount of my great misfortune.—
The little bells of heaven
Resound with joy;
The bells of the earth
Rang out by themselves;
The soul of the penitent
Ascended into heaven.

The Birth of Bernardo Del Carpio

Alfonso the Chaste was reigning
In the kingdom of León;
He had a beautiful sister,
Doña Jimena was her name.
None other than the Count of Saldaña
Fell in love with her,
And his love prospered, for the princess
Loved him in return.
Many times they were together
And no one suspected,
And from their many meetings
She went with child;
She brought forth a baby,
He was milk-white and scarlet;
They named him Bernardo
For his luckless fate;
While she was swaddling him
She bathed him in tears:
"Why were you ever born, son,
To so hapless a mother?
To me and to your father
You spell love and disgrace."
When the good king heard of it
He shut her up in a cloister,
And he had the Count imprisoned
In Luna of the Towers.

Bernardo Del Carpio Learns of His Father

In the court of Alfonso the Chaste
Bernardo lived at his pleasure,
Ignorant of the prison
Where his father was lying;
At this many were filled with sadness
But none told him the truth
Because the king had forbidden
Any mention of the thing.
Two ladies revealed it to him
Artfully and with cunning.
When Bernardo knew the truth
The blood soured in his veins;
Going out from where he was dwelling
He cried aloud his grief;
He dressed himself in black clothes
And went before the king.
Seeing him dressed in mourning,
The king spoke in this fashion:
—Can it be, Bernardo,
That you desire my death?
Bernardo said: —My lord,
Your death I do not desire,
But I grieve for my father
Who has been this long time in prison.
I crave your mercy, good king,
May it be granted this day.
Alfonso was seized with wrath
And answered him in anger:
—Go from my sight, Bernardo,
And never again be so bold
As to speak to me of this
Or it will be worse for you.
And I swear to you, I promise,
That for as long as I live
Not for one single day
Will your father leave that prison.
—My lord, you are king, you can do
As you please and as it suits you,

But you reward ill those who serve you
And would serve you still.
May God bestir your heart
Before long to release my father,
For I shall go in mourning
Until the day he is free.

The Complaint of the Count of Saldaña

The Count Don Sancho Díaz,
That lord of Saldaña,
Drenched are the prison walls
With the tears he sheds.
In his grief and solitude
He bewails his fortune
To his son Don Bernardo,
To Alfonso the King and his sister:
—These my sorrowful white hairs
Again and again remind me
Of the cheerless endless years
That I have passed in prison.
When I came into this castle
My beard was scarcely begun,
And now, for my transgressions,
I behold it long and white.
What neglect, my son!
How is it that my blood
Does not cry out in your veins
To lend help where it is needed?
No doubt you are detained
In your mother's footsteps,
And, being of the King's cause,
You must think ill of mine.
You are all three against me;
It is not enough for a wretch
To have such enemies,
He must have his own flesh turn against him.
All those who keep me here
Recount your deeds to me;
For whom do you amass honor
If not for your father?
Here I remain in these irons,
Since you do not set me free;
Either I am a bad father
Or you a bad son, to fail me.
If I offend you, forgive me,
For in words I find some relief,

26

For I shed tears, being old,
And you are silent, being absent.

First Romance *of the Seven Princes of Lara*

Now Castilians in anger
Ride out of Castile
To carry war to the walls
Of ancient Calatrava;
They smashed them in three places
Along the Guadiana;
Through one breach the Christians enter,
The Moors escape through the others
With curses for Mohammed
And his unholy sect,
And they flee with loud shrieks
High into the mountains.
Oh God, what a warrior
Was Rodrigo de Lara, that day!
For he killed five thousand Moors
And took three hundred captive.
If he had died at that time
What fame he would have left!
He would not have slain his nephews
The seven Princes of Lara,
He would not have sold their heads
To a Moor to take away.
Ruy Velazquez de Lara
Fought well on that day;
A rich tent from Arabia
And a bench of gold were his booty;
He sent them as a present
To the Count Garci Fernandez,
For him to arrange a marriage
With the fair Doña Lambra.
Now the wedding has been contracted
(Oh God, in an evil hour)
Between Doña Lambra de Bureba
And Don Rodrigo de Lara.
They held the marriage in Burgos
And the next day's feast in Salas;
At the wedding and the feasting
They spent seven weeks.

Well enough went the wedding
But not the feasting after.
They had summoned guests from Castile,
From León and from Navarre;
They came in such multitudes
That the lodgings could not contain them,
And the seven Princes of Lara
Had not yet arrived.
There, look there, they are coming
Across that level plain!
Their mother Doña Sancha
Rode out to receive them;
They kissed her on the hands
And she kissed their faces.
—Now that you are all here
I am happy that you have come,
And especially you, Almanzor,
Whom I have loved best of all.
To your horses once more, my sons.
And take your weapons with you,
For you must go and lodge
Out in Cantarranas.
In God's name, my sons, I beg you,
Do not go to the market-place,
For the people are crowded together
And there are bitter quarrels.
Now the Princes have mounted,
Now they have gone to their lodgings;
They found the tables laid
And meat there in plenty;
After they had eaten
They sat down to play at tables.
That fair Doña Lambra,
Indulging her fantasy,
Had arrayed high targets
Along the river-bed.
One hurled the spear, then another,
But none struck the mark;
Then came a nobleman
From Bureba the costly,
A mounted knight
With a short spear in his hand.
He spurred forward

29

And flung his spear at the target,
Calling out:—Love, ladies,
Each one as you are beloved!
For there is more worth in one knight
From Bureba the costly
Than in seven or seventy
Sprung from the flower of Lara!
Doña Lambra, when she heard him,
Was filled with delight;
—Oh cursed be the lady
Who would deny you her body!
Were it not that I am married
I would tender you my own!
Doña Sancha has heard her
And in sorrow answers her:
—Be still, Lambra, be still,
You should not say such things,
For today you were promised in marriage
To Don Rodrigo de Lara.
—Be still yourself, Doña Sancha!
You would do well to say nothing,
Having brought forth seven sons
Like a sow in a quagmire!
A knight who had reared the Princes
Overheard every word.
With tears streaming from his eyes,
In moral rage and anguish,
He went out to the palace
Where the Princes were.
Some were playing at dice,
Some were playing at tables;
Gonzalo stood apart
Leaning against a railing:
—Tell me, what sorrow brings you,
My tutor, what has made you angry?—
Gonzalo insisted so long
That at last his teacher told him;
—Only, I beg you, my son,
Do not go to the market-place.—
Gonzalo would not have gone,
But his horse would not stay;
He galloped to the market-place,

He asked for a spear,
He looked at the target
Which no one had yet struck down;
He stood up in the stirrups,
He brought it to the ground.
When he had struck it down
He spoke in this fashion:
—Love, love, shameless ladies,
Each one as you are beloved,
For there is more worth in one knight
Sprung from the flower of Lara
Than in forty or fifty
From Bureba the costly!—
Doña Lambra, when she heard it,
Stepped down in fury
And left the market-place
Without waiting for her attendants,
And went to the palace
Where Don Rodrigo was,
And went in at the door
And gave tongue to her complaint:
—I have a grievance, Don Rodrigo!
I might as well be a widow!
I am ill-cherished in Castile
By those who should protect me!
The sons of Doña Sancha
Have insulted me to my face,
They have said that they would cut my skirts
In a shameful place,
And put a distaff in my belt
And make me spin,
And fatten their falcons
In my dovecote.
If you let this pass unavenged
I shall become a Mooress
And carry my complaint
To the good king Almanzor.—
—Hush, hush, my lady,
Do not say such a thing,
I shall wreak full vengeance for you
Upon the Princes of Lara.
The web is in the frame,

Spanish Ballads

It will soon be woven;
Men born and yet unborn
Will speak of it forever.

Second Romance *of the Seven Princes of Lara*

On the mountains of Altamira
Which are called the ridge of the Arabs
Don Rodrigo was waiting
For his sister's sons.
They were not slow in departing,
But the traitor grumbled and fretted
Swearing a great oath
On the cross of his sword
That he would sever the soul
From whoever detained the Princes.
  It was their teacher who kept them,
Giving them good advice;
It was old Nuño Salido,
Who inspects the omens.
When he has counseled them all
He rides along with them;
Their mother accompanies them
For a full day's journey:
—Farewell, farewell, my sons,
May you come back to us soon!—
  Now they ride away from their mother.
In the pine grove of Canicosa
They saw unpropitious omens,
Not to be made light of:
At the top of a dry pine tree
They saw a golden eaglet
Tormented to death
By a treacherous sparrowhawk.
Don Nuño saw the omen;
—We shall come to no good on this journey.
Seven forces of Moors
Are waiting for us in ambush.
In God's name I beg you, my lords,
Do not cross over the river,
For he who crosses over
Will never come back to Salas.—
  In pure recklessness
Gonzalo answered him

33

(He was the youngest in days,
But a strong man in battle):
—Do not say so, my teacher,
For that is where we are going.—
And he clapped spurs to his horse
And crossed over the river.

Third Romance *of the Seven Princes of Lara*

Now those seven brothers,
The same who are called the Princes,
Who are called the Princes of Lara,
Have fought until they are weary.
They cannot lift their arms,
So great is their weariness!
And Viara and Galve,
Almanzor's generals,
Are stricken with sorrow;
They curse the Princes' uncle
For leaving to their deaths
Noblemen of such valor,
Men who are sons, moreover,
Of his own sister.
They bring them away from the Moors,
Who do not wish to kill them.
They take them to their tents,
They take away their weapons,
They have sent for bread to give them,
And they have sent for drink.
Ruy Velazquez saw it
And said to Viara and Galve:
—An ill thing you are doing,
Allowing them to live,
For if they should escape
I shall not see Castile again,
For they will take my life,
I shall be helpless against them.—
The Moors were filled with grief
When they heard what he said.
The youngest of the Princes
Spoke to him in anger:
—Oh false and fiendish traitor,
How vast is your perfidy!
You led us here with your host
To fight against the Moors,
The enemies of the faith,
And you have sold us to them,

35

And you urge them to kill us here.
May you get no pardon from God;
May He grant you no pardon ever
For today's heinous sin!—
The Moors answered the Princes,
This is what they said:
—We cannot decide how to treat you,
Oh Princes of great worth,
For if we should let you live,
Ruy Velazquez would go
To Almanzor, in Cordoba,
And he would become a Moor,
And they would give him great power,
And if he should send it against us
He would do us much injury,
For he is a man of great guile.
We will spare your lives and return you
To where the battle was;
Take arms and defend yourselves;
We are grieved at your ill fortune.—
The Princes have armed themselves;
They have returned to the field.
Commending themselves to God
They await the Moors.
The Moors, at the sight of them,
With loud cries rode against them.
Then was a bloody battle!
How well they defended themselves!
The Moors were in such numbers
That they could not make way against them;
But they killed two thousand and seventy,
Not counting those whom they wounded.
Don Gonzalo, the youngest of all,
Was the one who wrought most carnage:
So many Moors he slaughtered!
So dearly he sold his life!
They are exhausted with fighting,
They can move no longer;
Their horses have been killed,
Their lances and swords are gone,
And all their other weapons
Have been broken in pieces.
The Moors have taken them captive.

36

They have stripped off their breastplates;
They have cut off their heads.
Ruy Velazquez beheld it all.
Don Gonzalo, the youngest of the seven,
Was overcome with anguish
At the sight of his dear brothers
Losing the heads from their shoulders;
He took heart again,
He broke from the arms that held him,
He set upon the Moor
Who was doing that butchery,
He struck him such a blow with his fist
That he left him dead on the ground.
He took up the man's sword.
He has killed twenty Moors.
They seized him again at last
And they cut off his head.
When all the Princes were dead
Ruy Velazquez turned away
Toward Burueva, his home.
He considered himself avenged,
Having arranged
This peerless treachery.

Fourth Romance *of the Seven Princes of Lara*

(The *romance* is in the person of Gonzalo Gustios, the Princes'
father.)

    In sorrow I abide in Burgos,
Blind with weeping at my misfortunes,
Not knowing when the day rises
Nor when the night has come,
Were it not that with hard heart
Doña Lambra, who hates me,
Each day as the dawn breaks
Sends to wake my grief also:
So that I may weep for my sons
One by one, every day
She has her men throw
Seven stones at my window.

Doña Urraca Reminds the Cid of Their Youth in Zamora

Away, away, Rodrigo,
Arrogant Castilian!
You should not have forgotten
The good days that are gone
When you were armed and knighted
At the altar of Santiago,
When the King was your godfather
And you, Rodrigo, his godchild;
Your arms my father gave you,
Your horse my mother gave you,
Your golden spurs I buckled on you
To your greater honor.
I thought we would be married;
For my sins it was not to be!
For you married Jimena,
Count Lozano's daughter;
Where she brought you money
I would have brought you kingdoms;
You turned from a king's daughter
To marry a vassal's child.—
    Rodrigo, at her words,
Was stung with anguish:
—Away, away, my vassals:
You knights and men-at-arms,
For I have been struck by an arrow
Shot from that strong tower;
With no iron on its shaft
It has gone through my heart;
And there is no cure for it,
I know, but sorrow!

Romance *of the Cid: The Cid's vassals, mounting his*
body upon Babieca, defeat Búcar.

Dead lies that good Cid,
Rodrigo of Vivar.
Gil Díaz, his good servant,
Does as he was bidden.
He embalms the body;
He leaves it stiff and rigid;
Its face is beautiful,
Of great beauty and well colored,
Its two eyes equally open,
Its beard dressed with great care;
It does not appear to be dead,
But seems to be still alive,
And to make it stay upright
Gil Díaz proceeds with cunning:
He sets it in a saddle
With a board between its shoulders
And at its breast another;
At the sides these are joined together;
They go under the arms
And cover the back of the head.
So for the back, and another
Comes up as far as the beard,
Holding the body upright
So that it leans to no side.
Twelve days have passed
Since the death of the Cid.
His vassals armed themselves
To ride out to battle
Against the Moorish king Búcar
And the rabble he led.
When it was midnight
They placed upon Babieca
The body, prepared as it was,
And onto the horse they tied it.
It sits erect and upright,
It looks as though it were living,
With breeches on its legs

Embroidered black and white,
Resembling the hose he had worn
When he was alive.
They dressed it in garments
Adorned with needlework,
And his shield, at the neck,
Swung with its device.
A helmet on its head
Fashioned of painted parchment
Looks as though it were iron,
It was so well contrived.
In the right hand the sword Tizona
Was cunningly fastened;
It was wonderful to watch it
Go forward in the raised hand.
On one side rode the bishop,
The famous Don Jerome,
On the other Gil Díaz
Who guided Babieca.
Don Pedro Bermúdez rode forth
With the Cid's banner raised,
With four hundred nobles
In his company:
Then the main file advanced
With as many again for escort;
The Cid's corpse rode forth
With a brave company.
One hundred are the guardians
Who rode with the honored corpse,
Behind it goes Doña Jimena
With all her train,
With six hundred knights
There to be her guard:
They go in silence, so softly
You would say there were less than twenty.
Now they have left Valencia,
The clear day has dawned;
Alvar Fañez was the first
Who charged with fury
Upon the host of the Moors
Assembled with Búcar.
He found himself confronted
With a beautiful Mooress;

She was skilled at shooting
Arrows from a quiver
With a Turkish bow.
Star was what they called her
Because of her excellence
With the javelin.
She was the first who took horse
And rode forward
With a hundred others like her,
All valiant and daring.
The Cid's vassals charged them with fury
And left them dead on the ground.
King Búcar has seen them,
And the other kings who are with him.
They are filled with wonder
At the sight of the Christian host.
To them it looks as though
There are seventy thousand knights,
Each of them white as snow,
And one who fills them with dread,
Grown now more huge than ever,
Riding on a white horse,
A colored cross on his breast,
In his hand a white standard.
The sword looks like a flame
To spread carnage among the Moors;
Great slaughter it wields among them,
They flee, they do not wait.
King Búcar and the kings who are with him
Abandon the field;
They make straight for the sea
Where the ships were left
The Cid's knights charge after them.
Not one of them escaped.
All gasped and sank in the sea;
More than ten thousand drowned.
All rushing there together,
Not one of them reached the ships.
Of the kings, twenty were killed.
Búcar escaped by flight.
The Cid's vassals seize the tents
And much gold and much silver.
The poorest was made rich

With what they took there.
They set out for Castile
As the good Cid had commanded.
They have come to San Pedro,
San Pedro of Cardeña.
There they have left his body
Whom all Spain has honored.

2. *Single* Romances

Rosaflorida

In Castile there is a castle
Called Rocafrida,
The castle is called Roca
And the fountain Frida.
Its walls are of fine silver,
Of gold its battlements,
And in each embrasure
There is a sapphire set
Which shines abroad at night
Like the sun at noon.
    Within there was a maiden
Named Rosaflorida;
She had seven counts for suitors,
Three dukes of Lombardy,
And she scorned them every one,
So lofty is her pride!
She fell in love with Montesinos,
From hearsay, not from sight;
And in her passion
She cried aloud at midnight.
She was heard by a chamberlain
Who was there as her tutor.
—What is this, my lady,
What is this, Rosaflorida?
You must be tormented with love
Or else out of your senses!—
—Chamberlain, I bid you,
Carry my message.
Bear these letters for me
Into rich France.
Tell Montesinos,
Whom I most love,
To come to me
For Easter Sunday.
If he is unwilling
I will repay him.
I will clothe his squires

44

In scarlet apparel.
I will give him seven castles,
The finest in Castile.
Much more I will give him
If he desires more.
I will give him my body
Which has no peer for beauty
Unless it be for my sister's,
May bad fires consume her!
And if she is prettier
I am more fresh and graceful.

Count Arnaldos

Who ever will find such fortune
On the waters of the sea
As befell Count Arnaldos
On St. John's Day morning?
As he was going hunting
With his hawk on his hand
He saw a galley
Making in for the land.
Its sails were of silk,
Of fine silk its rigging,
The sailor at the helm
Came singing a song
At which the sea grew smooth
And the winds became gentle,
And the fish that go in the deep
Came swimming to the top,
And the birds that go flying
Came to perch on the mast.
Then spoke Count Arnaldos,
You will hear what he said:
—I beg you in God's name, sailor,
Repeat that song to me.—
The sailor made him answer,
This was his reply:
—I repeat that song to no one
But to him who comes with me.

The Fair Princess

There was the fair princess
In the shade of an olive tree,
With a golden comb in her hands,
Combing and combing her hair.
She lifted her eyes toward heaven
On the side where the sun rises;
She saw a file of armed men
Coming up the Guadalquivir,
In its center Alfonso Ramos,
Admiral of Castile.
—Welcome, Alfonso Ramos,
Good fortune attend your arrival,
And from my bristling fleet
What news do you bring me?—
—I have tidings for you, my lady,
If you promise to spare my life.—
—Speak out, Alfonso Ramos;
I promise that I will spare it.—
—Yonder the Moors of Barbary
Are overrunning Castile.—
—Had it not been for my promise
I would have seen your head fall.—
—Were you to cut off my head
It would cost you your own.

Meliselda

If you know the pains of love,
In your grace, in your goodness,
Knight, if to France you go,
Ask for Gaiferos,
And tell him that his lady
Commends herself to him,
That his jousts and tourneys
Are famous among us,
And his courtliness
At praising the ladies.
Tell him for a certainty
That they will wed me:
Tomorrow I must marry
One from across the sea.

Death and the Lover

Last night I dreamed a dream,
A little dream, from my soul,
I dreamed about my love,
That I held in my arms;
I saw a white lady enter,
White, whiter than the cold snow.
—Where did you come in, love?
How did you come in, my life?
The doors are closed, the windows,
The shutters.
—I am not love, young lover,
But Death, whom God has sent you.
—Ah Death, severe though you are,
One day of life grant me!
—One day it cannot be,
One hour only.
In haste he put on his shoes,
In more haste his clothes,
And now he is in the street
Where his love lives.
—Open the door to me, white love,
Open the door to me, girl!
—How should I open to you
When it is not time?
My father has not gone to the palace
Nor is my mother sleeping.
—Open to me this night
Or never, beloved;
Death is close behind me,
I would have life beside you.
—Go under the window
Where I stitched and embroidered,
I will throw you a silken cord
For you to climb;
If it does not reach to you
I will add my braided hair.
The fine silk has broken
And on the instant Death was there:

—Let us depart, young lover,
For the hour is over.

Cool Fountain

Cool fountain, cool fountain,
Cool fountain where love is,
Where all the little birds
Go and find solace,
Except the turtledove
Who is widowed and full of sorrow.
Near that place there passed
The nightingale, that traitor:
—Lady, if it meets your pleasure,
It is mine to serve you.
—Away, be gone, tormentor,
Evil one, false one, deceiver,
For I perch neither on green bough
Nor in flowering meadow,
For if I find the water clear
Turbid I drank it,
For I desire no husband,
For I want no children, no,
Nor to take pleasure in them,
Nor any consolation.
Leave me, wretch, enemy,
Evil one, false one, foul traitor,
For I will not be your mistress
Nor marry you either, no!

Fair Melisenda

Everyone was asleep
Who was in God's keeping,
But not Melisenda
The Emperor's daughter;
Love for Count Ayuelo
Would not let her rest.
She leapt out of bed
As her mother bore her,
She dressed herself in a smock,
For she could not find a shift,
She went through the palace
To where her ladies were;
Slapping them with her hand
She called out to them:
—If you are asleep, my maidens,
If you are asleep, come awake,
And you who know something of love
Be pleased to advise me,
And you who of love know nothing,
Keep this a secret for me.
Love for Count Ayuelo
Will not let me rest.—
Then spoke an old woman,
Old, aged, and ancient:
—While you are a girl, daughter,
See to it that you have pleasure;
If you wait until you are old
Not a boy will desire you.
This I learned as a girl
(And I cannot forget it)
At the time when I was a servant
In your father's house.—
When Melisenda had heard that
She waited to hear no more,
She went to find the Count
In the palace where he was,
She kept to the shadows of the eaves
So that no one should recognize her.

She met Hernandillo,
Her father's constable;
When he saw her walking alone
He began to cross himself:
—What is this, Melisenda,
What can this mean?
It must be that love torments you
Or else you are raving mad!—
—I am not tormented by love,
I pine for no one,
But once I had a sickness
When I was a child;
I promised to make a novena
There in St. John Lateran;
The ladies went in the daytime,
The maidens are going now.—
—When Hernando heard what she said
He answered nothing more;
But the enraged princess
Desired vengeance upon him:
—Now lend me, Hernando,
Lend me now your dagger,
For I am frightened, I am frightened
Of the dogs in the street.—
By the point he took his dagger
And handed her the hilt;
Such a stroke she gave him
That he fell dead to the ground.
—Now go, Hernandillo,
And report to the King, my father.—
And she went to the palace
Where Count Ayuelo was;
She found the doors locked,
And no way in;
With the art of enchantment
She flung open the doors.
Seven torches were burning there,
She put out every one.
The Count came awake
Filled with a great terror:
—Now God in heaven preserve me
And Santa María his mother!
Is it my enemies

Come to murder me,
Or is it my transgressions
Come to lead me astray?—
The cunning Melisenda
Began to speak to him:
—My lord, do not be alarmed,
Let fear have no place in you,
For I am a Moorish girl
Come from over the sea.
My body is as white
As a fine crystal;
My teeth are as tiny,
As tiny as salt,
My mouth is red
As a fine coral.—
Then spoke the good Count,
This answer he made her:
—I have made an oath,
I have sworn on a prayer-book,
Never to deny my body
To any woman who should demand it,
Except Melisenda
The Emperor's daughter.—
Then Melisenda
Fell to kissing him,
And in the black darkness
Their game is of Venus.
   When the morning came
And it began to dawn,
He opened the shutters
In order to see the Mooress;
He saw that it was Melisenda
And he spoke to her:
—Lady, it would have been better
If you had killed me last night
Before so great an evil
Had been committed!—
He went to the Emperor
To tell him of this matter;
Kneeling upon the ground
He began to speak:
—I have brought you tidings
That are sorrowful to tell.

But see, here is the sword
With which to take vengeance on me;
For last night Melisenda
Came into my palace;
She told me that she was a Mooress
From over the sea,
And that she had come to sleep
And to have her pleasure with me.
And then, wretched that I am,
I let her lie beside me!
Then spoke the Emperor
And make this reply:
—Put away, put away your sword,
For I wish you no injury;
But if you will have her, Count,
I will give her to you to marry.
Then the Count said:—I rejoice,
In my heart I am happy.
Whatever your Highness commands,
Here I am to obey.
They sent to fetch the bishop
To perform the ceremony;
They held rich celebrations
With great solemnity.

Tenderina

Dukes and counts are going
Into the King's palace;
An old count entered there
With his son by the hand.
Tenderina has called him
Behind the main altar:
—God be my protection, boy,
If you were twenty-one
You should eat with me at table
And you should sleep beside me.—
—If growth is all that counts, my lady,
I am as large as I need be.—
—Silence, boy, silence, boy,
For you would boast about it.—
—No woman ever gave me her body
And I boasted about it.—
But the next day in the morning
He boasted about it:
—Such ease I had in my bed last night,
It was a dream of pleasure,
For I slept with Tenderina,
The Count of Saragossa's daughter.—
—Silence, boy, silence, boy,
Oh ignorant boy;
If you have slept with a woman,
Her you shall marry.—
—With this sword let them kill me,
With this sword at my side,
If ever I marry a woman
Who gave me her body.

When the Moon Was As High

When the moon was as high
As the sun at midday
The good German Count
Slept with the Queen,
And no one knew of it,
No one in the court,
Except the Princess,
Her own daughter.
In this manner
Her mother spoke to her:
—Princess, whatever you saw,
Whatever you saw keep secret;
The German Count will give you
A mantle of fine gold.—
—A bad fire burn it, Mother,
That mantle of fine gold,
If I must have a stepfather
While my father is still living!—
Weeping, she went out from there
And met the King her father:
—Why are you crying, Princess?
Tell me, what made you weep?—
—I was sitting here at table
Eating bread soaked in wine,
And the German Count came in
And spilled it on my gown.—
—Hush, daughter, hush, daughter,
Do not let it trouble you,
For the German Count is only a boy
And he did it jesting.—
—Father, may a bad fire
Burn such laughter and jesting,
For he took me in his arms
And would have had his pleasure with me.—
—If he took you in his arms
And would have his pleasure with you,
Before the sun is in the sky
I shall send to take his life.

57

Knight, the Time Has Come

Knight, the time has come,
It is time we went from here;
I cannot stand up to walk,
Nor wait on the Emperor;
For my belly is swollen,
My garments will not meet around me,
I am ashamed before my maidens
Who have to dress me,
They catch one another's eyes,
They never stop laughing;
I am ashamed before my knights
Who serve in my presence.
—I say give birth to it, lady,
As my mother did me;
For I am the son of a laborer
And a bread-vendor bore me.—
When the Princess heard what he said
She cursed and railed:
—Curses fall on any maid
Who would bear such a man's child!—
—Do not curse yourself, lady,
Do not call down curses;
My father is the King of France,
Doña Beatriz is my mother;
I have a hundred castles
In France, lady, to house you,
Kept by a hundred damsels,
Lady, to serve you.

Lanzarote

The King had three little sons,
Three little sons and no more,
And out of anger at them
He cursed them every one.
One turned into a stag,
Into a dog, another,
And the other turned into a Moor
And crossed the ocean waters.
Lanzarote was walking
At leisure among the ladies;
One of them cried out to him:
—Stay, knight, oh stay!
If such might be my fortune
My fate would be fulfilled
If I were to be married to you,
If it pleased you to wed me,
And if, for my bride-gift, you gave me
That stag with the white foot.—
—With all my heart, my lady,
I would give it to you
If I knew the country
Where that stag was reared.—
Now Lanzarote has taken horse,
Now he has mounted, and now he departs.
With him, ranging before him,
Are his two hounds on the leash.
He has come to a hermitage
Where a hermit is living:
—God watch over you, good man.—
And a good welcome to you;
To judge from the hounds you have with you
It seems that you are a hunter.—
—You that live in sanctity,
Hermit, tell me:
That stag with the white feet,
Where does he stay?—
—My son, do not go from this place
Before it is day;

I will tell you what I have seen
And all that is known to me.
This last night he went past here
Two hours before dawn;
Seven lions were with him
And a mother lioness.
Seven counts are lying dead,
And of knights a great number.
God preserve you forever, my son,
Wherever you go,
For whoever sent you to this place
Hoped never again to see you.
Ah, Lady Quintañones,
May a bad fire burn you,
Since so many excellent knights
Have lost their lives for you!

The Mistress of Bernal Francés

I am all alone in my bed
Making love to my pillow;
Who could he be, this knight
Who at my door calls, "Open"?
—I am Bernal Francés, lady,
Who for some time have served you,
In your bed in the nighttime
And by day in your garden.
   She lifted back the Holland sheets,
She wrapped a shawl around her,
She took a golden candlestick
And went down to open the door.
No sooner was the door ajar
Than he blew out the candle.
—Our Lady keep me in her care,
And my lord Saint Giles protect me,
For He who has put out my candle
Could put out my life as easily!—
—Do not be frightened, Catalina;
I want no one to see me,
For I have killed a man in the street
And justice follows close behind me.—
She has taken him by the hand
And led him to her chamber,
And made him sit in a silver chair
With a back of ivory,
And she has bathed his whole body
With Balm Gentle water,
She has made him a bed of roses
And a bolster of gilliflowers.
—What is troubling you, Bernal Francés,
That you are sad as you lie there?
Are you afraid of justice?
The watch will not enter here.
Are you afraid because of my servants?
They are sound asleep.
—I am not afraid of justice,
For I seek it for myself,

Still less do I fear the servants,
Sleeping their sound sleep.
—What is troubling you, Bernal Francés?
You were never so before.
You have left another love in France,
Or someone has spoken ill of me.—
—I have left no other love in France,
For I never served another.—
—If you are afraid because of my husband,
He is far far away from here.—
—Far far away can become near
If a man wants to travel,
And as for your husband, my lady,
He is lying here beside you.
As a present upon my homecoming
I shall dress you in rich apparel:
I shall dress you in fine scarlet
With a red lining,
And such a crimson necklace
As I never saw on a lady;
I shall give you my sword for a necklace
To go around your neck.
And word will go to your Francés
That he can mourn for you.

The Fair Maid

You are more fair, my lady,
Than a ray of the sun;
Can I sleep this night
Disarmed and without fear?
For it has been seven years, seven,
Since I took off my armor;
My flesh is blacker
Than a sooty coal.
—You can sleep this night, sir,
Disarmed and without fear,
For the Count has gone hunting
To the mountains of León.—
—May his dogs die of rabies,
Eagles strike his falcons,
And his chestnut steed drag him
Home from the mountain.—
While they were talking
Up rode her husband.
—What are you doing, fair daughter
Of a treacherous father?—
—I am combing my hair, my lord,
And in great sorrow
Because you left me alone
And went to the mountains.—
—Your answer, maid,
Was false from beginning to end.
Whose is that horse
That neighed below there?—
—It comes from my father, my lord,
And he sent it for you.—
—Whose are those weapons
In the gallery?—
—They come from my brother, my lord,
He sent them today.—
—Whose is that lance
That I can see from here?—
—Take it, Count, take it,
And kill me with it,

63

Spanish Ballads

For such a death I merit,
Good Count, at your hands.

The Enchanted Princess

The knight has gone hunting, hunting,
As often before,
His hounds are weary,
He has lost his falcon.
Against an oak he leaned,
It was marvelously high;
On a branch at the top
He saw a little princess;
The hair of her head
Covered all of that oak tree.
—Knight, do not be afraid,
Nor draw back with dread,
For I am the good King's daughter,
My mother is Queen of Castile.
Seven fairies bewitched me
In my nurse's arms
To remain for seven years
Alone on this mountain.
It is seven years today,
Or at dawn tomorrow.
Knight, in God's name I beg you,
Take me away with you,
To be your wife if you please,
Or if not, your mistress.—
—Wait for me, my lady,
Until dawn tomorrow.
I will go to my mother nearby
And ask her to advise me.—
The girl gave him an answer,
These are the words she spoke:
—Oh knight, you are wrong and foolish
To leave me here alone!—
But he goes to get advice
And leaves her on the mountain.
The advice that his mother gave him
Was to take her for his mistress.
When the knight returned to the place
He could not find the Princess.

He saw a great procession
Bearing her away.
The knight, when he beheld it,
Fell down onto the ground,
And when he came to his senses
The words he spoke were these:
—The knight who could lose such a thing
Deserves a heavy penance:
I will be my own judge,
I will pronounce my own sentence:
Let them cut off my feet and hands
And through the town drag me.

Fresh Rose

Fresh rose, fresh rose,
Most fair and loving
When I had you in my arms
I did not know how to serve you,
And now when I would have you
I cannot serve you, no.
—You are to blame for that, friend,
You, and not me, no.
You sent a letter to me
Through a servant of yours
Who never gave it to me
But told me a different story:
He said you were married, friend,
There in the lands of León,
And had a wife of great beauty
And children like a flower.—
—Whoever told you that, lady,
Did not tell you the truth, no,
For I never set foot in Castile,
Nor there in the lands of León,
Except when I was little
And knew nothing of love.

Constancy

My ornaments are arms,
My repose is fighting,
My bed the hard stones,
My sleep endless watching;
The houses are dark,
The roads yet to travel,
Heaven with its changes
Delights to do me evil;
Going from crag to crag
By the shores of the ocean,
Seeking whether any place
Might ease my fortune.
But for you, my lady,
All must be borne.

The Prisoner

It was May, the month of May,
When warm days are with us,
When the grain gets its growth
And the fields are in flower,
When the skylark sings
And the nightingale gives answer,
When those who are in love,
Go in love's service,
Except for me, wretch, living
In sorrow in this prison,
Not knowing when it is day
Nor when night has come
Except for a little bird
Which sang to me at dawn;
A man killed it with a crossbow,
God give him an ill reward!

One Castle, Two Castles

There was a princess who held
One castle, two castles,
And there were twelve counts
Who all wanted to marry her,
And there was a squire of hers
Who waited upon her.
She said:—Squire, good squire,
You would do me great kindness
If you were to take this letter
To the knight of Encina,
And if he would come to see me
I would reward his journey
With garments worked with gold,
All worked with gold and fine silver;
If this should not content him
Another thing I would give him.
I would give him two castles
That look out on the sea,
And in the keep of each castle
A hundred men-at-arms,
With their wages in order
For a year and a day.
If he is still unsatisfied
I will give him myself besides.

The Corpse-Keeper

Seven years I have kept him, dead
And hidden in my chamber.
I change the shirt on him
Every holiday of the year.
I have anointed his face
With roses and white wine.
I have watched his bones laid bare
Of their white white flesh.
Alas, what can I do,
Wretch, in my disgrace?
Should I tell my father
He would say it is my lover;
Should I tell my mother
I would have no peace after;
Should I tell my sister
She knows nothing of love;
Should I tell my brother
He is the man to kill me;
Should I tell the constable
He would have me punished.
Better for me to say nothing,
To endure it and hold my tongue.
One day at my balcony,
Looking from my window,
I saw a huntsman passing
Who hunts in our crags.
—Huntsman, good huntsman,
One word, hear me:
Will you bury a dead body?
You will be rewarded.
And not in worthless coppers
But in gold and silver.—
Going down the stairs
Two thousand kisses I gave him:
—Farewell, delight of my life,
Farewell, delight of my soul;
It will not be long
Before I come and visit you.

Knight, Where Are You Going

Knight, where are you going,
Leaving me alone?
I have three little children
Who cry and call for bread.—
—I have left you fields and vineyards
And half of a city.—
—That will not suffice me
Nor provide me with bread.—
He put his hand into his breast
And gave her a hundred doubloons:
—If in seven years I am still gone,
In the eighth you must marry.—
His mother heard what he said
And she muttered a curse.
Time came and time went.
Remorse overcame her.
She went and stood at the window
That looked out on the ocean,
And she saw galleons
On the sea sailing.
—Have you set eyes on my son,
The child of my body?—
—I have seen your son,
The child of your body.
He had a stone for his pillow
And sand for his coverlet,
There were three knife-wounds in him,
The sun entered through one
And the moon through another;
In and out of the smallest
A sparrow-hawk was flying.—
His mother when she heard it
Would have leapt down into the sea.
—Do not throw yourself down, Mother,
For I am your own son.—
—If you are my own son
What proof can you give me?—
That little moon-shaped mark

Under your left breast.—
They clasped hand in hand
And fled away together.

Upon These Seas

Upon these seas sailing
As fortune bore me
I came to foreign lands
Where none knew me,
Where no cockerel crowed
Nor hen called aloud.
Where the orange grows,
The lemon, the citron,
And a vase of rue stands guard
Over the creature.
Ah Julián, false betrayer,
Author of my troubles,
You came into my gardens
And you deceived me!
Ah, you picked my flower,
You plucked it grain by grain!
Ah, with your delicate talk
And you deceived me!
Ah, and high-born as I was
They married me to Julián,
The gardener's son
From my own garden.
Ah Julián, let us go
From this unkind place;
Let rain fall down from heaven
Upon us.

There Was a Beautiful Lady

There was a beautiful lady,
No one was more lovely:
She wore frock upon frock,
A sumptuous skirt,
A blouse of Holland linen,
A tunic and collar of pearls.
Her forehead is dazzling,
And her hair is of brass,
Her brow mother-of-pearl,
Her eyes almonds,
Her nose fine as a feather,
Her cheeks roses,
Her mouth very rounded,
Her teeth pearls,
Slender her throat,
Pomegranates her breasts,
Her waist small, her body
Drawn fine like a cypress.
When she went in to hear mass
The church danced with light.
There the musician saw her
As he played on an instrument.
—Play on, play on, wretch—
As she kneeled down she said,
—For I have come for you,
Because the one I came for
Is not at mass, no.
Seven years I have waited for him
As an honorable woman.
After eight years without him
In the ninth I will marry.
Let the King of France take me,
Or the Duke of Stambul.
If the Duke will not have me
The musician can take me;
Let him play to me day and night
And sing to me at dawn.—

They clasped hand in hand
And went away together.

Face Like a Flower

   —Open the door to me,
Open it, face like a flower;
You have been mine since you were a child,
How much more so now.—
She with the face like a flower
Went down and opened the door;
They went to the garden
Hand in hand together.
Under a green rose tree
They set their table.
Eating and drinking
They fell asleep together.
When it was midnight
He awoke lamenting:
—What pain I have in my side,
Here in my side!—
—I will bring a learned doctor
For your healing,
I will give you a bag of money
For your spending,
I will bring you fresh bread
For your eating.—
—When you have killed a man
You talk of healing!

The Invitation

Mariana, I am invited
To a wedding on Sunday.—
—That wedding, Don Alonso,
Should be between you and me.—
—It is not my wedding, Mariana,
The groom is a brother of mine.—
—Sit down here, Don Alonso,
On this flowered bench
Which was left to me by my father
For the man who should marry me.—
Don Alonso sat down there
And soon he was asleep.
Mariana, in silence,
Crept out to the flowering garden.
Three ounces of corrosive,
Four of powdered steel,
The blood of three serpents,
A live lizard's skin
And the shin bone of a toad
She put into the wine.
—Drink some wine, Don Alonso;
Don Alonso, drink some wine.—
—After you, Mariana,
For that's as it should be.—
Sly Mariana
Poured it down her dress.
Don Alonso, like a young man,
Drank it at one draught.
So strong was the poison
That his teeth fell out of his head.
—What is this, Mariana?
What is this in the wine?—
—Three ounces of corrosive,
Four of powdered steel,
The blood of three serpents,
A live lizard's skin
And the shin bone of a toad
To deprive you of your life.—

—Good Mariana, cure me
And I will marry you.—
—Don Alonso, it cannot be
For your heart is cleft in two.—
—Farewell, bride of my soul,
Soon you will have no husband.
Farewell, Father and Mother,
Soon you will have no son.
When I left my house
On a piebald horse I rode,
And now I shall go to the church
In a box of pinewood.

King Ramiro and His Commanders

Now King Ramiro is seated,
Now he has sat down to dine;
Three of his commanders
Have appeared before him.
One is named Armiño,
Another is Galvane,
The third is Tello, wearing
The star of a commander.
—May God preserve you, my lord.—
—Commanders, you are welcome.
What tidings do you bring me
From the field of Palomares?—
—We bring you good news, my lord,
As we come from that place.
We journeyed seven days
And never ate bread,
Nor were the horses fed,
Which grieved us worse,
And we found no inhabited place
Nor a soul to speak to
Except for seven huntsmen
Who had gone hunting there,
And whether we would or no
We had to fight with them.
Four of them we killed,
Three we brought back with us.
Good King, if you do not believe us
They themselves will bear witness.

The Gray She-Wolf

As I was in my hut
Painting my shepherd's crook
The Pleiades were climbing
And the moon waning;
Sheep are poor prophets
Not to keep to the fold.
I saw seven wolves
Come up through a dark gully.
They cast lots as they came
To see who should enter the fold;
It fell to an old she-wolf,
Gray, grizzled and bow-legged,
With fangs lifting her lips
Like the points of knives.
Three times she circled the fold
And could take nothing;
Once more she went round it
And snatched the white lamb,
The Merino's daughter,
Niece of the earless ewe,
Which my masters were saving
For Easter Sunday.
—Come here, my seven pups,
Here, my bitch from Trujilla,
Here, you on the chain,
Run down the gray she-wolf.
If you fetch back the lamb
On milk and bread you will dine;
Fail to fetch her back,
You'll dine on my stick.—
On the heels of the she-wolf
They wore their nails down to crumbs;
Seven leagues they ran her
On the harsh mountains.
Climbing a little ravine,
The she-wolf begins to tire:
—Here, dogs, you can take the lamb,
As sound and well as ever.—

—We do not want the lamb
From your wolving mouth;
Your skin is what we want,
For a coat for the shepherd,
Your tail to make laces
To fasten his breeches,
Your head for a bag
To keep spoons in,
And your guts for lute strings
To make the ladies dance.

The Hill Girl

Mother, as I was going
To Villa Real
I lost my way
In a rough place.
Seven days I went on
And I ate no bread,
Nor my mule barley,
Nor my falcon meat.
Between Zarzuela
And Durazután
I raised my eyes
To the side where the sun rises;
I saw a little house
And smoke rising from it.
I spurred my mule
And traveled toward it.
Sheep dogs came out
To bark at my heels.
I saw a hill girl
Of exquisite grace:
—Come in, come in, sir,
Do not be shy,
My father and mother
Have gone to the village,
My lover Minguillo
Has gone for bread
And will not be back
Till tomorrow at supper;
You can drink milk
While the chese is making.
We will make our bed
In the broom together.
We will make a boy baby,
We will call him Pascual,
He will be an archbishop,
Pope, cardinal,
Or else a swineherd
In Villa Real.

In good faith, my joy,
You should be merry.

Up There on the Mountain

Up there on the mountain
There goes a shepherd weeping;
So many tears have spilled from his eyes
That his coat is drenched with them.
Do not bury me in holy ground
If I die of this pain,
Bury me out in the meadow
Where no flocks go past.
Let my hair lie outside the grave,
Carefully combed and curled,
So that those who pass by may say:
—Here he died in misery.—
There were three ladies who passed there,
All three of them weeping.
One of them said:—Farewell, my cousin!—
The next:—Farewell, my brother!—
But she who was the youngest
Said:—Farewell, my true love!

Catalina

I went soft about a girl
In my heart and soul,
They called her Catalina,
I can't forget her, no.
She pled with me to take her
To the lands of Aragon.
—You're still a girl, Catalina,
You can't travel, no.
I'll go as far, as far, sir,
And a-foot, as you will go.
If money's what dissuades you
I'll bring enough for two,
Ducats for Castile
And florins for Aragon.—
And the constables surprised them
As they were talking so.

The Cock and the Vixen

Vixen, you're out early
In this nasty weather.—
—No, friend, none too early
When you think what I'm out for.
In my right cheek here
I've a tooth that's killing me.
If you would pull it for me
I'd do you some other favor.—
—Close your eyes, then, vixen.—
And the cock flew onto the roof-tree.
—Cock-a-doodle come down, come down!
Come down, cock crow!—
—The first time that you caught me
You pulled out all my tail,
And the next time you won't leave me
With a whole bone in my body!

My Mother Made Me Marry

My mother made me marry.
When I was pretty and little,
A rogue, a boy,
Whom I didn't love at all.
When it struck midnight
Out went the rogue,
Cloak on shoulder
And his sword slung on.
I followed his footsteps
To see where he would go,
And I saw him enter
His lady-love's house.
I went close to listen
To hear what he would say
And I heard him tell her:
—For you, my little dove,
I intend to purchase
Petticoats and shawls,
And I'll give that other woman
A stick and bad times.—
I went back home
In sorrow and dismay.
I sat down to eat
But eat I could not,
I sat down to sew
But sew I could not,
I got down to pray
But pray I could not.
I went to the balcony
To see if he was coming.
I heard his footsteps
Coming up the street.
He came to the door
And he called out and said:
—Open to me, open to me,
Open the door, love,
For I've come home weary
From making us a living.—

—You've come home, liar,
From your lady-love,
I distinctly heard you tell her:
—For you, my little dove,
I intend to purchase
Petticoats and shawls,
And I'll give that other woman
A stick and bad times.

The Garland

Daughter, that garland of roses,
Who gave it to you?—
—It was given me by a knight
Who went past my door;
He came and took me by the hand
And led me to his house;
There in a dark little doorway
He had his pleasure with me.
He laid me on a bed of roses
Where I had never lain before;
What he did to me I cannot say,
But what he did I love him for.
Mother, I have got my shift
Stained with blood all over.—
—Oh terrible catastrophe!
Oh, my wits are reeling!
If what you say is true, daughter,
Your honor is not worth a thing,
For people talk maliciously
And goodbye to your reputation.—
—Mother, Mother, say no more,
My dear mother, be still;
Better a good lover
Than to be married and married ill.
For my part give me a good lover,
A good cloak and petticoat, Mother,
For she is a miserable creature
Who has a bad husband to cover her.—
—If that is as you prefer it, daughter,
If that is your pleasure, I want no better.

Mathathias Weeping at the Destruction of Jerusalem

   —Alas!—said the good father
To his five sons,
—Why should I have survived
To behold this day?
In my soul's sorrow to see
The holy city
In the hands of the enemy
Who slaughter without mercy
Old people and children
And plunder wherever they can,
And enforce sacrifice
To their idolatry.—
In his grief he rose up
As though to worship
And by his own hand perished
On the altar where he lay.

Don García

  Don García is walking
Along the top of a wall,
With arrows of gold in one hand
And a bow in the other.
He calls down curses on Fortune,
He recounts her abuses:
—When I was a child the King reared me,
God was a cloak around me;
A horse and arms he gave me
Excelling all others;
He gave me Doña María
To be my wife and consort,
He gave me a hundred maidens
To wait upon her,
He gave me the Castle of Uraña
As her dowry,
He gave me a hundred knights
To keep the castle,
He provided me with wine,
He provided me with bread,
He provided me with sweet water,
For there was none in the place.
The Moors laid siege to me there
On St. John's Day in the morning.
Seven years have come and gone
And the siege has not been lifted.
I have seen my people die
Because I had nothing to give them.
I set them up on the ramparts
With their weapons in their hands
So that the Moors should think
That they were ready for battle.
In the Castle of Uraña
There is only one loaf of bread.
If I give it to my children
What then of my wife?
If I were so base as to eat it
They would not forgive me.—

He broke the bread into four pieces
And flung it down into the camp.
One of the four pieces
Rolled to the King's feet:
—Allah, here is grief for my Moors!
Allah is pleased to afflict them.
From his castle's overabundance
He supplies our encampment!—
And he bade them sound the trumpets
And they lifted their siege.

Romances *of Valdovinos*

i

The moon is as high
As the sun at noon
As Valdovinos comes forth
From the aqueduct of Seville.
There he happened to meet
A pretty Moorish girl;
Seven years Valdovinos
Had her for his mistress.
At the end of seven years
Valdovinos heaved a sigh.
—Did you sigh, Valdovinos,
My love, whom I most love?
It must be that you fear the Moors
Or love another mistress.—
—Neither do I fear the Moors
Nor still less love another mistress,
But with you Moorish and I a Christian,
We lead a life of wickedness:
It is like eating meat on Friday,
My law forbids it.—
—For love of you, Valdovinos,
I will become a Christian,
To be your wife, if you choose,
Or if not, your mistress.

ii

Through the aqueduct of Carmona
Where the water flows to Seville,
There went Valdovinos
And his pretty mistress
Feet in the water,
One hand on his armor,
For fear of the Moors,
Lest they should be spied.

Mouth to mouth they joined,
With none to forbid them;
In dismay Valdovinos
Heaved a sigh.
—Why do you sigh, my lord,
My heart and my life?
It must be that you fear the Moors
Or have a mistress in France.—
—Neither do I fear the Moors
Nor have I a mistress in France,
But with you Moorish and I a Christian
We lead a most wicked life:
We eat meat on Friday,
Which my law forbids.
It is seven years, seven,
Since last I heard Mass.
If the Emperor knew of it
It would cost me my life.
—For love of you, Valdovinos,
I would become a Christian.—
—And I, lady, for you,
A Moor among Moors.

3. *Historical* Romances

The Siege of Baza

The King was beside Baza
Monday, after he had dined;
He looked at the proud tents
Of the army's encampment;
He looked at the spreading fields
And the outlying hamlets;
He looked at the heavy parapet
Girdling the city;
He looked at the thick towers,
Too many to be counted.
A Moor behind a battlement
Called out to him:
—Go somewhere else, King Fernando,
Do not spend the winter here,
For the weather of this country
Will be more than you can bear.
We have bread enough for ten years,
A thousand beeves for salting
We have twenty thousand Moors here
All capable of fighting;
We have eight hundred horsemen
To ride out skirmishing;
We have seven nobles
Each one as valiant as Roland,
And each of them has sworn
To die rather than yield.

Romances *of the Siege of Baeza*

i

   Moors, my young Moors,
You that win my sustenance,
Break down Baeza for me,
That towered city;
And its old men and old women,
Put them all to the sword,
And its young boys and young girls,
Let the riders carry them off,
And Pedro Díaz's daughter
To be my beloved,
And her sister Leonor
To keep her company.
Go, Captain Vanegas,
The greater honor be yours,
For if I send you
I am sure of your return,
And that you will not suffer
Indignity or outrage.

ii

   That Moor Andalla Mir
Has laid siege to Baeza.
Eighty thousand foot
And ten thousand knights are with him,
And with him is that traitor,
That traitor Pedro Gil.
At the Gate of Bedmar
They begin the fighting;
They set ladders to the wall,
They begin to prevail,
They have taken one tower,
No one can resist them.
Then from the tower of Calonge
I saw fighters come out.

97

Ruy Fernandez goes in front,
That intrepid chief;
He attacks Andalla,
He closes in to strike him,
He has cut off his head;
The rest take to flight.

The Ancient and True Romance *of the Siege of Alora*

Alora, the well surrounded,
You that are by the river,
The Governor went to besiege you
On a Sunday morning.
With foot-soldiers and men-at-arms
The field was well furnished;
With the great artillery
He has made a breach in your wall.
You would have seen Moors and their women
Fleeing into the castle,
The women carrying clothing
And the men flour and wheat,
And the Moorish girls of fifteen
Carrying fine gold,
And the little Moorish boys
Carrying figs and raisins.
They had flown their banner
From the peak of the wall.
There was a young Moor posted
Behind a battlement
With a bolt ready in his crossbow
And his crossbow drawn.
He called with a loud voice
So that the people heard him:
—A truce, Governor, a truce!
The castle surrenders to you!—
The Governor lifts his vizor
To see who had addressed him.
The bolt was aimed at his forehead,
It came out through the back of his skull.
Pablo led his horse by the reins,
Little James took his hand,
Those two whom he had reared from children
In his own household.
They took him to the surgeons
To see whether they could heal him.
The first words that he uttered
Were his will and testament.

The King of Aragon

The King of Aragon looked out
One day from Campo-Viejo,
He looked out on the Spanish sea
Where the tides fall and rise,
He looked at the ships and galleys
Departing and arriving,
Some were vessels from the fleet,
Others merchantmen,
Some take the route for Flanders,
Others for Lombardy,
Those that come from the war,
How gallant their appearance!
He gazed upon the great city,
Naples is its name,
He looked at three castles
Of that great city,
Castelnuovo, Capuana,
And Santelmo, shining,
Shining out among them
Like the sun at noon.
He wept from his eyes
And he said:—Oh city
How dear you have cost me,
To my great sorrow!
You have cost me counts and dukes,
Men of great worth,
You have cost me a brother
Dear as a son to me,
And of the others, the common soldiers,
Beyond count or comparison.
Twenty-two years you have cost me,
The best years I shall see,
For in you my beard darkened upon me
And in you it has turned gray.

4. *Moorish* Romances *and* Romances *of Captives*

Julianesa

—Move on, dogs, move on!
May you die of the rabies!
Thursday you kill the hog
And you eat his flesh on Friday.
Alas, seven years today
I have walked this valley,
Whence my unshod feet,
My nails running blood,
The raw flesh that I eat
And red blood I drink,
In sorrow seeking Julianesa,
The Emperor's daughter,
Whom the Moors stole from me
On St. John's Day morning, early,
Picking roses and flowers
In an orchard of her father's.—
Julianesa has heard him,
In the Moor's arms where she lies;
The tears from her eyes
Down the Moor's face fall.

Reduán

I am certain that you must remember,
Reduán, the promise you made me
To take the city of Jaén
In one night and give it to me.
Reduán, be as good as your word
And I shall double your pay,
But should you fail to do it
I will banish you from Granada
And send you to the frontier
Where you cannot enjoy your lady.—
    With unmoved countenance
Reduán answered:—If ever
I said it I have forgotten,
But I will keep my promise.—
    He asked for a thousand men,
The King gave him five thousand.
A great cavalcade rode out
There through the Gate of Elvira:
So many Moorish nobles,
So many bay mares,
So many gripped lances,
So many white bucklers,
So many green robes,
So many scarlet coats,
Such feathers and pageantry,
So many crimson cloaks,
So many fawn buskins,
So many handsome bowknots,
So many golden spurs,
So many stirrups of silver!
All of them valiant fighters
And veterans in battle,
And in the midst of them rode
The Boy King of Granada.
    The Moorish ladies were watching
From the towers of the Alhambra.
His mother, the Queen of the Moors,
Spoke to him in this manner:

—Allah preserve you, my son,
Mohammed be with you and keep you
And bring you back from Jaén
Free, unharmed, and in triumph,
And send you peace with your uncle
The lord of Guadix and Baza.

Fragment of a Romance

(It was on the Eve of the Kings . . .)

It was on the Eve of the Kings,
The first holy day of the year,
When the son of the Moorish King
Begged a boon of his father.
I ask for no gold, no silver,
No luxury,
But for twenty thousand men
To ride out behind me.
Let no goats be left, no sheep,
No shepherd with his flock . . .

Altamare

The King of the Moors had a son,
They called him Taquino:
He fell in love with Altamare,
His own dear sister.
When he saw that it could not be
He took to his sickbed.
There his father paid him a visit
On a Monday morning.
—What ails you, son Taquino,
What ails you, child of my soul?—
—Father, it is a fever
Which has pierced my soul.—
—Shall I roast a bull for you,
One that we have reared ourselves?—
—Father, roast a bull for me
But let my sister serve it to me,
And let her when she comes to me
Come by herself with no company.—
And as it was in summer
She was wearing white petticoats.
As soon as she came in at the door
Like a lion he bore down on her
And he seized her by the hand
And back upon the bed he forced her
And took his joy of that fair lily
And that freshly budded rose.
—Let punishment descend from heaven
Since there is none on earth!—
—Upon my father let it fall
For he has been the cause of it all.

The Moorish King Who Lost Granada

The Moorish King was riding
Through the city of Granada,
From the Gate of Elvira
To the Gate of Vivarrambla,
   Alas for my Alhama!
Letters had come to him to say
That Alhama had been taken;
He threw the letters into the fire
And killed the messenger.
   Alas for my Alhama!
He got down from the mule he was riding
And he mounted a horse;
Up to the Zacatín
He rode to the Alhambra.
   Alas for my Alhama!
When he came into the Alhambra
He commanded them
To blow upon their trumpets,
Their long horns of silver.
   Alas for my Alhama!
And to beat upon the war drums
A quick call-to-arms
So that his Moors should hear it
In Vega and Granada.
   Alas for my Alhama!
All the Moors who heard the sound
Which summons to bloody Mars
One by one and two by two
Formed up in a great array.
   Alas for my Alhama!
Then spoke a venerable Moor,
He spoke in this manner:
—King, why have you sent for us?
What is this summons for?—
   Alas for my Alhama!
—You must be acquainted, my friends,
With a new calamity:
Christians of great bravery

Have taken from us Alhama.—
> *Alas for my Alhama!*

There spoke an elder
With a long beard and gray hair:
—That's just as you deserve, good King,
Good King, that's what you deserve!
> *Alas for my Alhama!*

You killed the Abencerrajes,
The flower of Granada;
You laid hands on the renegades
From renowned Cordoba.
> *Alas for my Alhama!*

For what you have done, King, you deserve
The heaviest penalty:
You deserve to lose your life and kingdom
And here to lose Granada!—
> *Alas for my Alhama!*

Governor of the Moors

Governor of the Moors,
You with the fine beard,
The King has sent to seize you
For the loss of Alhama.
—If the King has sent to seize me
For the loss of Alhama
The King will have his way,
But I owe him nothing.
For I had gone to Ronda
To my cousin's wedding
And had left behind in Alhama
The best guard I could muster.
If the King lost his city
I lost everything that I had;
I lost my wife and children,
The things which I most loved.

The Mooress Morayma

I was the Mooress Morayma,
A Moorish girl, and pretty;
A Christian came to my door,
Alas for me, to deceive me.
In Moorish speech he addressed me,
And he knew it well:
—Open the door to me, Moorish girl,
Allah keep you from evil.—
—Open to you, oh wretch that I am.
Not knowing who you may be?—
I am the Moor Mazote,
You own mother's brother;
I have killed a Christian,
The constable is close behind me;
Unless you let me in, my life,
You will see them kill me here.—
Alas for me, when I heard this
I rose up from my bed,
I threw a little cloak around me,
Not finding my silk shift;
I went over to the door
And I opened it all the way.

Then the Two Kings Sat Down

Then the two kings sat down
And the white Moor made three
And the white girl with them.
Then they sat down to play,
To play their game of chess.
One plays, the other plays,
They play all three.
Then the white Moor wins,
He wins once, he wins twice,
He wins three times.
—Why are you weeping, white girl?
Why are you weeping, white flower?
If you are weeping for your father
He is my jailer,
If you are weeping for your mother
She is my cook,
If you are weeping for your brothers
I have killed them all three.—
—I am not weeping for my father, my mother,
Nor for my three brothers.
I am weeping only
For my own fortune.—
—Your fortune, my lady,
Is here at your side.—
—If you are my fortune, give me
That little knife of cypress wood.
I will send it to my mother
So that she can rejoice at my fortune.—
Hilt first the white Moor gave it to her.
The white girl took it, turned it,
And buried it in her breast.

My Father Was from Ronda

My father was from Ronda,
My mother from Antequera;
The Moors took me prisoner
Between peace and war,
And they bore me off to sell me
At Jerez de la Frontera.
Seven days and their nights
I was there at auction;
Not a Moorish man nor woman
Would give money for me
Except for one dog of a Moor
Who gave a hundred gold pieces,
And to his house took me
And snapped a chain on me
And he gave me a foul life,
A black life he led me:
Pounding hemp by day,
By night milling fodder
With a bit in my mouth
Lest I should eat any,
And my hair in a knot,
And I went round on a chain.
But as pleased God in heaven
He had a kind housekeeper:
When the Moor went hunting,
From the chain she released me
And in her lap took me
And picked the lice from my head;
For a favor that I did her
One far greater she did me:
She gave me the hundred gold pieces
And sent me back to my country,
And thus it pleased God in heaven
That I came to safety.

The Three Captive Girls

By the green, green,
By the green olive,
There my three girls
Were taken captive.
The sly Moor
Who captured them
To the Queen of the Moors
Delivered them.
—What are the names
Of these three captives?—
—The eldest Constanza,
The next Lucia,
And the youngest of all
They call Rosalia.—
—What tasks shall we give
To these three captives?—
—Constanza to knead,
To sift, Lucia,
And the youngest of all
To fetch them water.—
One day, fetching water
From the cold fountain,
She met an old man
Who was drinking there.
—Good old man, what brings you
To the cold fountain?—
—I am waiting to see
My three captive daughters.—
—Then you are my father
And I am your daughter.
I must go and tell
My little sisters.—
—Let me tell you, Constanza,
I must tell you, Lucia,
How I met Father
At the cold fountain.—
Constanza wept
And Lucia sighed

But the youngest of all,
Hear what she said:
—Do not cry, Constanza,
Do not sigh, Lucia,
For the Moor, when he comes,
Will give us our freedom.—
The sly Moorish woman
Who overheard them
Opened a dungeon
And put them in.
The Moor, when he came,
Let them out again,
And to their poor father
Delivered them.

Epitaph of Albayaldos Sarracino

This trophy hanging
From the branch of this pine tree
Was Albayaldos Sarracino's
Who had no peer for bravery
Among the Moors of Granada.
Could Alexander make his way
To this sepulcher, he would weep,
Stung with more anguish and envy
Than when he wept at the grave of that Greek
Whom great Homer had sung.

5. *Late Lyric* Romances

Fragment of a Romance

I must tell you how it was with me
When I was in love:
My nights were misery,
Worse were my days,
In my mistress's service,
To win her sympathy.

That Shepherdess, Mother

That shepherdess, Mother,
With the blue eyes,
Ah God, she consumes my soul
Which is snow, and her eyes are fire!
When I make bold to adore her,
Well content with a poor reward,
She is a sea to my will
And a cliff to my desires.
But at the sight of those mountains,
Since my grief is assured,
Humbly and not in pride
I try to make myself heard;
But seeing that she is stone
I return to my troubled silence.

Hope Has Bidden Me Farewell

Hope has bidden me farewell,
Reward I see none,
Pleasure does not know me,
I do not lack for sorrow;
Where most I desire joy
There grows my torment;
None except days of sadness
Ever dawn for me;
The clear light of the sun
Darkens before my eyes.
In me the anguish of love
Never slumbers, though its cure
Sleeps to forget the glory
Which my sufferings deserve.
Death keeps me company
And offers herself hourly
But if I say:—Kill me—
She vanishes instantly
Rather than put an end
To my miseries, alas for me!
And the sense of my suffering
Grows numb and faints away,
But yet my will is not weakened
With my faith to sustain it.

Girl with the Dark Hair

Girl with the dark hair
If you are asleep, be warned:
Half of our life is a dream
Which runs and slips by us,
As rapid in its flight
As a light sleep wakened,
As brief while we are young
As when age is upon us,
For the sad disclosure
Of our fleet career
When it would wake us comes
Late and avails us nothing.
Your youth and beauty are
No more than a new merchant,
Rich to be left poor
By the lapse of time;
A glory of the world
And a veil for the eyes
And chains for the feet
And fetters for the fingers;
A ground for hazards,
A midden of envy,
A butcher of men,
A famous thief of time.
When death has shuffled
Ugly and fair together
In the narrow sepulcher
The bones do not know each other.
And though the cypress is higher
And the cedar more lovely, neither,
Burned into charcoal, is whiter
Than charcoal from the ash tree.
For in this woeful existence
Delight comes to us in dreams only
And distress and tribulation
When we are widest awake.
Dry autumn will consume
The flower of fresh April,

To unloved ivory
Turning your ebon hair.

Tirsis

—Where are you, my lady,
Untouched by my sorrow?
It is either unknown to you, lady,
Or else you are false and disloyal.
Once you took pity upon me
When my wounds were little,
Now when they are mortal
You are not moved at all.
How can you ease me in small things
And in great ones fail me?
For in the gravest dangers
Friendship is found out
And the crucible of truth
Is adversity.
What round of memory
Renders you deaf to my weeping?
I can remember (when sorrows
Will let me remember)
How, on an alder trunk
By the bank of the Tagus,
When I was more fortunate
And you were more constant and true,
You wrote, with your hand, one day:
"I give you my liberty.
The Tagus will leave its bed
Before I turn from you."
Roll back your water, river,
For faith departs from its word.—
Such was the theme of Tirsis
As he sang alone
Memories of his lady,
Proofs of his sorrow.

Oh Pale Maiden

Oh pale maiden,
Sadness has faded
The rose of your face
In the April of your days.
All the village wonders
At such melancholy;
Such suffering, they say,
Is of the soul, not the body.
If such is your condition,
If your bewitching eyes
Which once killed with joy
Are now dead with sadness,
If you never go out to the dancing,
And to you the tambourine
Sounds like a knell tolling
And a bell at a burying,
If when all the girls
Go out into the fields
For cresses and to plunder
The young almonds of their kernels
You remain in your little house
In a lightless room
So that even when the sun shines
You are clouded over,
Who will fail to say
That you suffer on your left side
And are little seen because
You merit no better acquaintance,
That I leave you and seek my pleasure
Where I have none,
Often stealing away
In scorn of quiet nights,
That I ill-treat your soul
And that you are worse to your body
Since to purge it of love
You dose it with desire?
Come awake, my girl,
Wake out of your deep silence,

For the village speaks ill of me
And so do your father's eyes.
I have green slippers waiting for you
For the day when you set
Your fair foot on the floor,
And my mouth awaits you.
A little gown of light crimson
Will cover your body
Which more than four covet
As do I, who possess it.
You will have earrings of crystal
Which I pray you not to break
For words are of crystal, and those
Which I give I do not break.
And if still you will not recover
Your health, you for whom I lose mine,
Then give me the illness, my lady,
Or let us share it between us,
For if you must be ill I would rather
That I were the sufferer;
Not you, who are my soul,
But I, who am your body.

That Village Beauty

That village beauty
From the plain of Madrid
With eyes dark and unsmiling,
Her waist and her body graceful,
She who knows of my torments
And is pleased to behold them,
Not so that she may restore me
But merely to watch me dying,
From a little mountain of roses,
Orange blossom and balm gentle,
She sallied forth to steal hearts
In the April mornings.

6. *A Wonder-Mongering* Romance

A Rare and Miraculous Case

You gentlemen lend me your ears
And do not be amazed,
And all you timid women,
Do not take fright at this:
It came to pass in Ireland,
As is true beyond a question,
That there was a poor woman
Who went to ask for alms,
She had many children with her,
They were beautiful to see;
She came to beg for money,
To provide them all with food,
From Doña Margarita,
A princess, as they say,
Without peer in that country.
When she saw so many children
She asked that poor soul:
—Are all those your own children?—
And she was answered thus:
—Yes, my lady, by one father,
Who's still living, at your service.—
—Impossible—she answered,
For I am very certain
That they're children of many fathers
As you cannot deny.—
The poor soul was afflicted
At being slandered so,
She raised her hands to heaven
And kneeled down on the ground,
And she said:—Oh may it please God,
Who can do it if He will,
To send you so many children,
My lady, by one father,
That you won't know one from the others,
Nor be able to bring them up!—
This prayer was so acceptable
That that lady brought to birth

Three hundred and sixty children;
It was indeed a marvel!
They were all born in a single day
In pain, but with no danger,
Like little mice, they were so small,
And alive without exception.
And in a font of silver,
And by a bishop, they
Were every single one baptized,
And afterwards they went to taste
That glory which has no compare
Beyond all estimation.
That very font unto this day
In a church has been preserved,
And it was put upon display
To Charles our emperor.
And authors of great merit
To the truth of this will swear,
One is Baptista Fulgoso,
And Enrico, with Algozar,
And Doctor Vives of Valencia,
Who is not to be ignored.

Bibliography and Notes

The most important modern student of the *romances* is Don Ramón Menéndez Pidal; anyone who takes pleasure in these poems and tries to find out something about them falls rapidly into his debt. Not only has he collected them himself for years, but his works on the tradition of the *romances*—their origin, their place in the life of the people who made them and who handed them down from generation to generation, their development, their variation, their distribution, etc.—have contributed enormously to the modern interest in and understanding of the *romances*. For readers who know Spanish, his large volume on the *Romancero Español*, his *Poesía Juglaresca y Juglares*, and his *De Primitiva Lírica Española y Antigua Épica* are standard works, authoritative, rich in information, and the last two at least are easily obtainable (in the *Colección Austral.*)

The collections from which I have made these translations are the following:

1. *Flor Nueva de Romances Viejos*—Ramón Menéndez Pidal, Colección Austral—Buenos Aires—Espasa Calpe. 1948.

2. *Romancero Español*—por Luis Santuellano, Selección de Romances Antiguos y Modernos, Según las Colecciones Más Autorizadas. Aguilar, Madrid. 1946.

3. *Romancero General*—Colección de Romances Castellanos Anteriores al Siglo XVIII—por Don Agustín Duran—2 volumes—Biblioteca de Autores Españoles—Madrid. 1945.

4. *Romancero Popular de la Montaña*—Colección de Romances Tradicionales Recogido y Ordenados por José Mª de Cossio y Tomás Maza Solano—Sociedad Menéndez y Pelayo—Librería Moderna, Santander.

5. *Romances de Tradición Oral*—José M. de Cossio—Colección Austral—Espasa Calpe, Buenos Aires.

126

6. *Antología de Poesía Española*—by Damaso Alonso y J. M. Blecua.

7. *Romancero del Cid*—M. E. Aguilar—Colección Criso—Madrid. 1944.

There are also selections of the *romances* in the *Oxford Book of Spanish Verse* and in the *Penguin Book of Spanish Verse*, the latter accompanied by prose translations.

For those who may want to use the present versions in order to get closer to the original poems I append a list of textual sources for these. Where the same text occurs in several collections I have mentioned the most easily available one. In the list the collections which I have named are referred to as follows:

FN   *Flor Nueva de Romances Viejos*
RE   *Romancero Español*
RG   *Romancero General*
RM   *Romancero Popular de la Montaña*
RTO   *Romances de Tradición Oral*
APE   *Antología de Poesía Española*
OB   *Oxford Book of Spanish Verse*
RC   *Romancero del Cid*

The first number in each case refers to the poem's number in the Table of Contents of this volume.

1. FN (As the pagination of this collection and of the *Romancero General* has changed from printing to printing, I have not given page numbers for the poems from these collections.)
2. RE, variant FN
3. FN
4. FN
5. FN
6. FN
7. RE
8. FN
9. FN
10. RE
11. FN
12. FN
13. RC p. 466
14. RE, FN
15. OB p. 72
16. OB p. 65
17. RE
18. FN
19. OB p. 71, FN
20. composite of variants in FN and RE
21. RE
22. RE
23. RE
24. OB p. 65
25. FN
26. OB p. 70, variant FN
27. many variants; OB p. 73, FN, and others in other collections

28. OB p. 71
29. OB p. 70
30. FN (a variant: OB p. 72)
31. RE
32. RE
33. RE
34. RE
35. RE
36. RE
37. RE
38. RG vol. 2 p. 214
39. FN
40. APE p. 4
41. RE
42. RG vol. 2 p. 450
43. RTO p. 130
44. RE
45. RE
46. RE
47. RG vol. 2 p. 215
48. RE
49. RE

50. RE, OB p. 59
51. FN
52. RE
53. OB p. 69, variant FN
54. FN
55. RM
56. RE
57. OB p. 63, FN
58. RG vol. 2, p. 89
59. OB p. 64, FN
60. RE
61. OB p. 64
62. RE
63. RG vol. 2 p. 119
64. RG vol. 2 p. 448
65. RG vol. 2 p. 491
66. RG vol. 2 p. 431
67. RG vol. 2 p. 419
68. RG vol. 2 p. 487
69. RG vol. 2
70. RG vol. 2 p. 508
71. RG vol. 2 p. 393

Eufemia / Lope de Rueda

Characters

LEONARDO, *a gentleman*

MELCHIOR, *a serving man*

EUFEMIA, *Leonardo's sister*

XIMENA DE PENALOSA, *a nurse*

CRISTINA, *serving maid to Eufemia*

POLO
VALLEJO } *servants to Valiano*

GRIMALDO, *a page*

PEDRO, *an old servant*

VALIANO, *a baron*

A GIPSY

EULALLIA, *a negress*

LEONARDO: Oh, how interminable this past night seemed to me. I suppose that was because of the unease of mind in which I went to bed in the small hours of this morning. It must have been that, because it's a long time since I heard my dear sister, Eufemia, talking with the servants. For she, too, went away to her sleep troubled by the same thoughts, when she found she could not dissuade me from making this journey. I wonder whether Melchior has done what I left him last night to do. Melchior! Ho, Melchior!

MELCHIOR: Quick, quick! The Moors are invading the place. And me with my craw crammed when he wants an answer.

LEONARDO: Melchior! The devil take that donkey! Where is he, that he doesn't hear me?

MELCHIOR: Don't hear, you say? By God, if I wanted to I could hear him before he called. Well, what's the flurry? For I lace up my interests as well as any man of honor. Throw this Melchior a supportative and you'll see how brisk I am with him.

LEONARDO: You mean superlative, bell-dong.

MELCHIOR: Just so, senor. What were Ximena de Penalosa and I racketing about the other day?

LEONARDO: I don't remember.

MELCHIOR: Don't remember that we nearly fell to beating each other because she told me to my beard that the Penalosas as a lineage were superior to the Ortizes?

LEONARDO: All right, I remember.

MELCHIOR: Glory be to God! Well now to save it from simplicity, prompt that Melchior with some little thing at the beginning and you'll see what will happen.

LEONARDO: Ah! Senor Melchior Ortiz?

MELCHIOR: Now I'm content. What does your lordship desire?

LEONARDO: God strike you sore for requiring such terminology before you'll come.

MELCHIOR: Not for my own larding; just so that that sinful crone can hear how I'm honored out of your worship's very mouth. I'm content with a "hey, you"; it more than suffices, it overwhelms me like the sea.

LEONARDO: And what has all this to do with her?

MELCHIOR: She says she's better than my mother, when there's not a man or woman in all my village who ever opens his mouth without praising her higher than the bees did the bear.

LEONARDO: There's respect, indeed.

MELCHIOR: And for what? A woman in whose past nobody has ever found so much as one single clot.

LEONARDO: You mean blot.

MELCHIOR: Whom all the world praises. Isn't that enough, senor?

LEONARDO: Well, I don't know what they say thereabouts of her doings.

MELCHIOR: Nothing to say. What could they say? She was a little thievish, as God and all the world know, and somewhat lewd with her body. As for the rest, wasn't she . . .what do they call those leather things they fill with wine, senor?

LEONARDO: Wineskins.

MELCHIOR: Can't your worship think of another name?

LEONARDO: Drunkards.

MELCHIOR: She was that way, too; and as for that you could as safely trust her with a pile of gold as you could a new-delivered she-cat with a yard of sausages, or me with a pot of stew. She'd collar it all for the pot.

LEONARDO: So much for your mother. And your father, was he an official?

MELCHIOR: Senor, he was, they say, one of the governing body of Constantina de la Sierra.

LEONARDO: What office?

MELCHIOR: Name me the public trusts.

LEONARDO: Mayor.

MELCHIOR: A little bit lower.

LEONARDO: Constable.

MELCHIOR: He wasn't a constable; he had only one eye.

LEONARDO: Bum-bailiff.

MELCHIOR: He was no good at running, since they'd cut off one foot out of justice.

LEONARDO: Scrivener.

MELCHIOR: In our entire ancestry there was not a single man who could read.

LEONARDO: Well, what office did he hold?

MELCHIOR: What do you call those people who carve one man up into four?

LEONARDO: Hangmen.

MELCHIOR: Hangman, hangman, that's what he was; and chief keeper of the kennels in Constantina de la Sierra.

LEONARDO: Son of an honored father!

MELCHIOR: And how dare Senora Penalosa pretend she's worthy to live with my shoe, since we're all children of Adrian and Esteban?

LEONARDO: Be still for a minute. Your mistress is coming. Go!

EUFEMIA: Abroad so early, Leonardo, my dear brother?

LEONARDO: My most dear Eufemia, today, if God may be served thereby, I wish to begin my journey to those parts where I may serve him.

EUFEMIA: Ah, are you still determined to set out without knowing where you are going? How cruel! Even though you are my brother I cannot understand you. Ah, luckless me! When I think of your decision and firm resolve, it conjures up before me the death of our beloved parents. Oh, brother! You should remember how your father and mine, when he was dying, commended me into your charge because I was a girl and younger than you. Don't go, Leonardo; have pity on your disconsolate sister, who with all reason entreats you, still commending herself into your hands.

LEONARDO: My dearly beloved Eufemia, not even your pious tears can impede my departure, on which I have been resolved for so long, and from which only death could turn me aside. I can only beg you to behave as wise and virtuous maidens do when they have been deprived of the shelter and guidance of parents. I have no other advice to give you, except that wherever I may be you will be visited by my letters. And for now, while I go to hear Mass, see that this lackey does what I ordered him to.

EUFEMIA: Go, brother, and good fortune go with you; and in your prayers beseech God to grant me that resignation which I shall need to endure your absence.

LEONARDO: I shall. God be with you.

EUFEMIA: Ortiz! Ah, Melchior Ortiz!

MELCHIOR: Senora?

EUFEMIA: Come out here. You're needed.

MELCHIOR: Coming, coming; don't say any more. I've hit what it is already.

EUFEMIA: Well, if you know what it is, do it and be quick, for your master's gone to hear Mass and will be back before long.

MELCHIOR: I don't know where to start.

EUFEMIA: As long as you get it all done, begin where you like.

MELCHIOR: Oh God, all right: in the name of God . . .; but does your ladyship know what I would like?

EUFEMIA: No, since you haven't told me.

MELCHIOR: To know where I'm going, or what for.

EUFEMIA: What did your master tell you to do last night before he went to bed?

MELCHIOR: The things he told me—

XIMENA: My soul, my bowels from which I wish you well, oh, if I've been able to sleep one hour out of this whole night.

EUFEMIA: What was the matter, nurse?

XIMENA: Mosquitoes, so be-jabbing me in my conscience you'd think I were a stick to swarm bees on.

MELCHIOR: The lady should sleep with her mouth open.

XIMENA: Whether I sleep at all or not, what is it to this frog-face?

MELCHIOR: How can the lady hope not to be had by mosquitoes if out of the week's seven days she spends eight imitating a wine-vat?

XIMENA: Oh, senora! Did your ladyship hear what he just said, this gruel-spoon, right in the middle of my face? Oh! Please God to feed you sour grapes.

MELCHIOR: Sour grapes? Nobody would even understand the lady's curses.

XIMENA: Why not, mould for blockheads?

MELCHIOR: How can the lady bottle-basket bring me sour grapes if she's always ripening into wine?

XIMENA: Oh, be bold, Don Vagabond, if I don't pay you out for this!

MELCHIOR: Move on, face of a mule with the gripes.

XIMENA: Oh, senora! Your ladyship, let me lay hands on that hop-kettle. Do you see how he works me, this offal-stitcher?

MELCHIOR: Flap for a tavern, procure, procure, alley-corner, rig for a scarecrow.

EUFEMIA: Gently, gently; what's this? Are we to have no manners at all? In whose presence do you think you are?

CRISTINA: Oh, my lady! Isn't there a stick to take to this wallow-pig? May I never be saved if you wouldn't have said from out there that there was a cane-tourney going on, from the noise.

EUFEMIA: It's true, they go on like a cat and dog when they're together.

CRISTINA: In good faith you'd be better employed, Senor Melchior Ortiz, in seeing to that nag; it's three days now, and the saddle hasn't come off him.

MELCHIOR: Sister Cristina, I marvel at what you say. How in the Devil's name could it come off him with the crupper and both the two cinches tight as garrottes to hold it frozen on to him?

EUFEMIA: Deliver me from the wiles of the evil one! Does it seem to you a good thing to leave the poor nag for three days without taking the saddle off? He'll be in a fine state for traveling.

XIMENA: There's looking after his lord's possessions.

MELCHIOR: Possessions? Do you think that if I weren't overflowing with good will I'd have done that for the nag?

CRISTINA: And does leaving it for three nights with its saddle on strike you as the part of careful solicitude?

MELCHIOR: By God, sister Cristina, I'm a liar if I left him with his clothes on for any reason but so that he could use his new saddle and bridle for a salt lick. Worse evils he's suffering than the support of this blessing.

EUFEMIA: Oh heavens! What?

MELCHIOR: Well, since my master came back from the grange the day before yesterday, a curse light on the least grain of barley he's tasted at my hands.

EUFEMIA: God preserve me! And you wait until now to tell me. Run, Cristina; see if it's true.

MELCHIOR: As true, senora, as that I'm the son of Gabriel Ortiz and Arias Carrasco, executioner and chief keeper of the kennels in Constantina de la Sierra.

XIMENA: Honored titles, your father's.

MELCHIOR: God give me the like, amen.

EUFEMIA: Your ambition's huge indeed.

MELCHIOR: Senora, you may take it for gospel that when my father was about the hanging of anybody he was no more swayed by justice than if it had never come near him.

CRISTINA: Oh, senora, what a catastrophe! Look, your ladyship; how was the poor nag to eat with the bridle and all in his mouth?

EUFEMIA: The bridle?

MELCHIOR: Yes, senora, the bridle, the bridle.

EUFEMIA: And you left him bridled, you Judas?

MELCHIOR: It is my station to be a diviner, or would my breeding lead you to think I'd serve my master as badly as that?

EUFEMIA: How would it harm him to unbridle his nag?

MELCHIOR: When it was my master who bridled him wouldn't you call it the depths of disservice and a scandal to my name if I undid what my lord had done?

XIMENA: What rhetoric you please, he'll have an answer to it.

MELCHIOR: Rhetoric? I sucked it in with my mother's milk.

EUFEMIA: Was she so learned, your mother?

MELCHIOR: By God, senora, almost any night when she got up from table, no magpie or thrush in a cage was ever half a match for her gabble.

CRISTINA: Oh, senora! Please come in, your ladyship. We must make shift to do what we can, for my master will be back any minute now and he'll want to start right away.

EUFEMIA: Quite true. Let's go in.

XIMENA: Let the model servant go first.

MELCHIOR: No, after the trusty squire.

II

POLO: I must be early, since none of the others who were supposed to come are here yet. And what's the good of getting here ahead of time just to hold up this raver Vallejo's honor? Oh, he's a heroic engine, that man; there's not a day goes by in the whole week that he doesn't set the lackeys of the house, or part of them, in an uproar. Now look how the Devil he's got himself imbroiled with the choir-deacon's page, Grimaldo, who's one of the best behaved fellows in the place. So now I have to watch and see how far he can heave his pike and stretch his soul, since he lays claim to so much valor.

VALLEJO: Oh, what suffering must be borne in this world! How can one endure such a thing, especially at the doorway of the cathedral, where so many people of quality are always coming and going. Is it possible that a bare-faced boy born yesterday should affront me to my beard, and then that my master's lackeys should tell me to keep still because his master the choir-deacon is a friend of the man who maintains me? I would as soon walked naked from here to Jerusalem with my feet bare and a toad in my mouth crawling over my teeth,

as leave such a business uncastigated. Here's my comrade.
Ah, Senor Polo! Have any of these boyos arrived yet?

POLO: I haven't seen anybody.

VALLEJO: Excellent. Senor Polo, you must do me this grace: even
though you should see multitudes arrive, you must fold your
cloak and sit down on it, and be improved by my example
in this matter of settling disputes. And if you see several
bodies fall dead at my feet—and pleasing the Divine Majesty,
there can be no fewer—keep a lookout for the law while I
make my escape.

POLO: What? How's that? Has poor Grimaldo sinned so mortally
that you would bring yourself and your friends to such a
pass?

VALLEJO: What more does Your Grace want, Senor Polo, when
at the turn, as he was bearing his master's, the choir-deacon's
train, he trod on the hem of my livery-cloak? Was anyone
ever so affronted and had not before this point laid out a
dozen and a half men in mummy-meat?

POLO: For a little thing like that? God bless me!

VALLEJO: Little? When he laughed in my face afterwards like a
joker?

POLO: Well, Grimaldo is an honest fellow all the same, and I'm
amazed that he'd do such a thing; but he'll come and acquit
himself, and you, senor, will forgive him.

VALLEJO: How can you say it? I'm oppressed by our friendship
which makes me countenance such a speech. If I should
forgive this affair, tell me, which one would you have me
press on with?

POLO: Ssh, softly. Here he comes.

GRIMALDO: Well, gentlemen, it's time we embarked on this affair.

POLO: I've been begging Senor Vallejo to proceed no further with
this business, but his heart's so set on it, my words had no
weight at all.

GRIMALDO: If Your Grace will walk to one side, we'll see what
this fighting-cock's made of.

POLO: Now, my lords, let me say one thing and this is it: I'll
stand in the middle and see whether you won't do me the
signal grace of not fighting, at least for now.

VALLEJO: Though you were to put me in front of all the artillery
pieces that are set to defend all the frontiers of Asia, Africa
and Europe, along with that serpentine bronze cannon which
to its over-weening arrogance has been dug up in Cartagena,
and for the same purpose resuscitated the wrought iron bom-

137

bards with which that Most Christian King Don Fernando took Baza, and lastly that illustrious Galleon of Portugal with all the men-at-arms it mustered, yet not all that I have mentioned and enumerated would suffice to turn me from my resolve.

POLO: Good Lord, senor, you frightened me. I was expecting no less than for you to mix up the Grand Turk's galleys with all the others that sail between the Levant and the Ponient.

VALLEJO: What? Didn't I mix them? Well, I give you them now in full tangle; let them come.

GRIMALDO: Senor Polo, why wait for such an arsenal? Leave this thief to me and let us get started.

VALLEJO: What thief, dribble-chin?

GRIMALDO: You. Who else am I talking to?

VALLEJO: Oh, what a cross to bear! To have this beardless shaver treat me with familiarity!

GRIMALDO: As for me, rabbitguts, I've no need of a beard to deal with a chicken like you. I'll use yours instead, in the presence of Senor Polo, to wipe the soles of my shoes.

VALLEJO: The soles, Senor Polo! What would that incomparably gallant Spaniard, Diego Garcia de Paredes, have said?

GRIMALDO: As if you knew, gabble-mouth.

VALLEJO: I, peach-fuzz! You've heard of the combat of the eleven against the eleven in the Piedmont? Who survived it but he and I?

POLO: You, Your Worship? Is it true about that combat?

VALLEJO: What a question! And though a number of them at last downed him because he was tired, who dispatched them but this arm you see here?

POLO: Bless me, what a wonder!

GRIMALDO: It's a lie, Senor Polo. As though a man like Diego Garcia would keep company with a thief like this.

VALLEJO: Was I a thief then, pigeon?

GRIMALDO: If you weren't then, you are now.

VALLEJO: How do you know, gosling?

GRIMALDO: How? Tell us what happened to you in Benevente, where the story's thicker than weeds.

VALLEJO: Oh, I see your drift. Senor Polo, I'll recount it to you, for Your Worship understands these affairs of honor, and I'm not accustomed to giving satisfaction to fleas of this variety. I, senor, went to Benevente on a trifling matter: no more than the killing of five lackeys of the Count there; and I'd have you know why: because they'd turned a young woman against me with whom I'd found favor in her father's house in Medina del Campo.

POLO: I know that country well.

VALLEJO: After they were buried, and while I was still in hiding, finding myself somewhat in need, I fell to coveting a priest's mantle and a few tablecloths from a public-house where I used to eat, and the law laid hands on me, and in all truth and holiness, senor, *etcetera*. That's what this lad was referring to. And does my master now starve me because I once had resort to such means?

GRIMALDO: Come along, I'm in a hurry.

VALLEJO: Senor Polo, will Your Worship loosen these braces of mine a little?

POLO: Wait a moment, Senor Grimaldo.

VALLEJO: Now tighten up this lace next to my sword.

POLO: Is that better now?

VALLEJO: Now straighten the amulet which you'll find here beside my heart.

POLO: I can't find any amulet.

VALLEJO: What? Is my amulet not there?

POLO: Not a sign of it.

VALLEJO: Oh, I must have forgotten it; left it at home under the upper end of the pillow. I can't fight without that. Wait for me here, half of a mouse.

GRIMALDO: Come back here, coward.

VALLEJO: You can persist. It's only because of my amulet that I'm letting you live a bit longer. Senor Polo, for the ease of my conscience there are certain questions I must put to this boy.

POLO: Questions?

VALLEJO: Duty compels me, Your Worship. Has it been long, hedge-swallow, since you've been to confession?

GRIMALDO: What's that to you, cutpurse?

VALLEJO: Senor Polo, would Your Worship like to ascertain whether this poor lad has some message he'd like to send to his father, or wishes to have any Masses said for his soul?

POLO: Oh, I know his father and mother well, and the house where he lives, brother Vallejo, in case anything should happen to him.

VALLEJO: Ah. What's his father's name?

POLO: What does that have to do with it?

VALLEJO: I must know who will come looking to avenge his death.

POLO: Don't be ridiculous. You know his name is Luis de Grimaldo.

VALLEJO: Luis de Grimaldo?

POLO: Yes, Luis de Grimaldo.

VALLEJO: What have you said?

POLO: Nothing more than that.

VALLEJO: Then, Senor Polo, take this sword and plunge it as deep as you can into my right side, and after you've executed that judgment I'll explain why.

POLO: I, senor? God prevent me from doing such a thing, depriving somebody of his life who never did me any harm.

VALLEJO: Then, senor, if you my friend refuse me, we must seek out a certain man of Piedrahita, almost a third of whose family I've killed with my own hands, so that he can avenge his mortal enmity and bury his rage in my very body.

POLO: What for?

VALLEJO: What for? Did you not say that this is the son of Luis de Grimaldos, constable-in-chief of Lorca?

POLO: And no other.

VALLEJO: Oh, woe is me! Who is it that saved me from the noose times without number but this gentleman's father? Senor Grimaldo, take this dagger and with your own hands open my breast and take out my heart, and cut it down the middle and there you will find written the name of your father, Luis de Grimaldos.

GRIMALDO: What is all this? I don't follow you.

VALLEJO: I would not have killed you, by God's saints, for all the money my master gives me. Let's go, for I wish to devote what life remains to me to the service of this gentle youth, in recompense for the words which I uttered in my ignorance.

GRIMALDO: Enough of that, brother Vallejo. I'm quite ready to give you satisfaction in any way you like.

VALLEJO: On, I say! Let us go and take our new-found amity into the house of Malata the publican. I've four *reales* here; I'll not save a single coin, I tell you, but spend it all in the service of my more than master, Senor Grimaldos.

GRIMALDO: Many thanks, brother; keep your *reales* for your own occasions. The choir-deacon, my master, will be returning to the house. But I'll be ready if ever you decide you must clear your honor.

VALLEJO: Senor, command me as the least of your servants, and God be with you. Senor Polo, did you notice what a gallant lad he is?

POLO: He seems an honest fellow. Let's go; it's late. Who stayed to look after the mule?

VALLEJO: The groom did. Oh, Grimaldo, Grimaldo, how narrowly you escaped death by revealing to me who you were! But take care; never provoke me again, not by the least little jostle, or not all the parentage of the Grimaldos will save your poor wretched soul from my hands; no, though the mother's milk were not dry on your lips, I would not spare you.

III

MELCHIOR: Leonardo! Oh, praise God for returning you to me! Do you call that a nice trick to play on me? Is that the good company you promised before we left the place where we belong, as my lady Eufemia asked you?

LEONARDO: What did she ask? I don't remember.

MELCHIOR: Didn't she beg you to keep me good company?

LEONARDO: Well, what ill company have you received at my hands today?

MELCHIOR: Trust a man to be there when you get back, and then have to go prowling for more than seven hours like a slinking dog, without finding a trace of him either for good or ill.

LEONARDO: Couldn't you have gone back to the inn when you didn't find me?

MELCHIOR: Without a copper to give to the crier?

LEONARDO: The crier? What for, donkey?

MELCHIOR: So he could cry me for a lost beast and lead me from pillar to post till he found the place where we were lodging.

LEONARDO: Are you so half-witted that you couldn't find your way back to the inn?

MELCHIOR: If I'd found it would I be asking for my breakfast now?

LEONARDO: What? Not eaten yet? Impossible!

MELCHIOR: Not a word. My craw's as limp as a falcon's when they've kept him a whole day fasting.

LEONARDO: How in the Devil's name did you get lost this morning?

MELCHIOR: Well, as Your Worship was engaged in talking to that friend of yours, who as far as I was concerned was not a man but a disaster, I wandered a little to one side in case you were discussing anything secret, and I no more than turned my head to look at a tray of pastries a boy was carrying on his head, and when I looked back there were two other people in front of me, and as true as can be, one of them looked like you from behind, and they both slipped into the Cathedral to hear a Mass which they say goes on for an hour and a half, and I behind them, thinking it was Your Grace: and when they got around to saying *benelicamus dolime*, where the others answer *don grasilas*, I went up to the one who looked like you and said to him "Hoy, senor! How long before we go home?" And he turned his head and looked at me and said "Who are you, brother?"

LEONARDO: Oh, to have seen it!

MELCHIOR: So when I saw that that case was hopeless, I started back out to look for you, but for my sins which are forever making fun of me, I found that all the doors were shut.

LEONARDO: What an Odyssey!

MELCHIOR: Let me tell you. Has Your Worship ever seen a mouse that's fallen into a mousetrap go dashing around butting his head against one end after the other, looking for a way out?

LEONARDO: Yes, more than once.

MELCHIOR: Well, not a whit different was the plight of the luckless Melchior Ortiz Carrasco, until fortune favored me with a chink of a postern down in one corner where I noticed a few stragglers sneaking in to hear that Mass, which was the last.— But let's go, senor, since we're going.

LEONARDO: Where?

MELCHIOR: Where? Home.

LEONARDO: Home? At this hour? What for?

MELCHIOR: To put a little salt and wild marjoram in my mouth, senor.

LEONARDO: Why salt and wild marjoram?

MELCHIOR: Just to pickle my pipes.

LEONARDO: How?

MELCHIOR: Senor, they're marinaded already with pure hunger; the salt and wild marjoram will be something for them to be going on with, if it seems good to Your Worship.

LEONARDO: Well, we can't do it now. I've just noticed Valiano, the lord of this town; he's gone to Vespers, where I must join him. Come along; you'll hear the most solemn voices you ever heard in your life.

MELCHIOR: Senor, nothing could delight me more. Still, if I could be excused from hearing voices, it would be an overwhelming favor.

LEONARDO: Ah, villain, this will teach you to half-famish my poor hack. Remember?

MELCHIOR: Alas, Your Grace, though I sinned against God, punish the sin where I committed the pleasure; don't leave me here on a chance street-corner where nobody cares if I starve.

LEONARDO: All right; be quick: follow this street to the end and ask for the Wolf Tavern. Here's the key; you can eat what you find in the room, and wait in the inn until I get back.

MELCHIOR: Now there's an improvement in Melchior's condition. What leftovers are there waiting for me?

LEONARDO: Get along; you'll have no cause to complain.

MELCHIOR: I'm off. God grant I don't.

POLO: God keep Your Worship.

LEONARDO: Well met, Polo.

POLO: Tell me, are you the stranger who arrived a few days back accompanied by a manservant who comes from these parts?

LEONARDO: I'll answer to that. Why?

POLO: Because last night at table they were talking about your wit and intelligence, and how elegant Your Grace was with a pen, and what an excellent story-teller you were; and in short your accomplishments would be more than appreciated in the exercise and fulfillment of the office of secretary to Valiano, my master; who, because he's young and still unmarried, does not yet enjoy the full complement of servitors befitting his lands and station. It would delight me if Your Worship would stay here in the service of my lord, for I am sure your virtues would make you one of the ornaments of the local gentry.

LEONARDO: I should indeed be delighted to remain; especially since a certain knight whose name I don't know, whom I met by chance a day's journey from here, when he learned my intention, which was to enter into the service of some lord such as you describe yours, out of his courtesy directed me to this place. Furthermore, since I have in fact no endowments whatever except those of writing and telling stories, which my parents, be it said to their glory, taught me when I was a child. I asked that same gentleman to mention me to your lord, if by any chance such accomplishments might be of use to him.

POLO: Indeed, senor, by your decision you give evidence of being someone whose merits exceed even what is said of you. But I believe they're out looking through the town for you. Go to the Palace, Your Grace, where they're expecting you, for it wouldn't be right to let so excellent an opportunity slip past. Confirm it at once; we shall all be eager to do you service.

LEONARDO: My thanks; I'm grateful for that. I shall go now.

POLO: God be with you. As for me, I'll take a turn down this way and see if I can't catch a glimpse of the negress Eulallia, my doxy.

IV

VALIANO: Leonardo, I asked you to come out armed at this hour, not out of any concern for my own safety, but simply so that I might discuss with you that matter which I broached yesterday, and that's why I've brought you through streets so littered with people. And I've bidden my lackey, Vallejo, fetch cloak and sword and stand at the street corner to keep a close watch so that no one can contrive to overhear us.

LEONARDO: Vallejo?

VALLEJO: Who goes there? And where are they going? Death to the traitors!

VALIANO: Softly, softly. Who have you seen? What's the matter with you?

VALLEJO: Oh, sinner that I am, senor Valiano. What's to be gained by your sallying forth and putting your person in peril? Go, senor; you and Leonardo go to bed and leave them to me, and before dawn I'll have sent them to the oaks of Mechualon to be bait for sparrow hawks.

VALIANO: Go to the Devil! Pour some oil on your waters. Who'd molest me in my own domains?

VALLEJO: Oh! Curse the rig they use to hunt pigeons in Calabria. How can you say such a thing, senor? Can't you see that it's night, as I'm a sinner before God, and in the dark all is confusion. On my faith, if I hadn't recognized Senor Leonardo's voice, these lands by this time would be without an heir.

VALIANO: You'd turn your hand against me, traitor?

VALLEJO: Not unless I were surprised in my sleep! But walkers by night had best announce themselves, senor, for my fate is in my own hands and in That Power's which yoked the great horizon with its arctic and antarctic poles, and fixed it in its place with two cords.

VALIANO: If only you wouldn't get drunk so often.

VALLEJO: I must endure this, since you're my lord. But had anyone else said it, he'd be sitting down with the saints by this time.

VALIANO: Wait here, then, and see that no one eavesdrops on our conversation, for we've highly secret matters to discuss.

VALLEJO: You say that to a man like me? No, not though the ostrich-footed monster with all his hirelings should come down this street snapping like a pair of tongs, would it make me so much as move my right foot from where I'd planted it.

VALIANO: That will be a great help. Leonardo, to return to our subject; this sister of yours, apart from the beauty which you describe, is she modest and gentle of demeanor?

LEONARDO: Senor, it would be better for you to find out for yourself than for me to tell you; for since I am, after all, so intimately concerned in such an affair, my opinions should not be admitted on the same footing with everyone else's. Her chief defect in my addition must be that she is my sister; otherwise I would say that she might, for her qualities, be a worthy match for a lord of whatever rank.

VALLEJO: Senor Leonardo?

LEONARDO: What is it, Vallejo?

VALIANO: See what the fellow wants, Leonardo.

VALLEJO: Senor, I thought I heard you touch on something to do with women, and if that's the case, by the four elements of the unspeakably profound earth, there is not a man alive at this moment in all the world's rotundity who is such an expert on that subject as I am, nor as experienced.

VALIANO: How's that, Vallejo?

VALLEJO: Whom, senor, could so aptly discharge for you an affair of this sort as I could?

VALIANO: Why?

VALLEJO: Is there in all the whirling world, and I include the entire astrological machine, anyone to whom the fair creatures are as susceptible as they are to Vallejo your lackey?

VALIANO: Hold your tongue, wretch!

VALLEJO: Make no mistake, senor; if you knew what I know of the world, be your rank as may be, you might call yourself blessed if you were as favored in love as I.

VALIANO: And whom might your conquests include?

VALLEJO: Ah, that ill-fated Catalinilla from Viscaya! In Cadiz I wrested her from the power of Barrientos, sub-bo's'n on the galley from Grifo, for there wasn't a damsel in all that fleet more lusciously assembled.

LEONARDO: Brother Vallejo, do hush for a minute.

VALLEJO: I only mentioned it because we were discussing battle-axes.

VALIANO: Be still, do you hear?

VALLEJO: God forgive you, Leonore de Balderas! Now there was a girl to have fed a whole army.

VALIANO: What Leonore was that?

VALLEJO: The one whom I snatched from Corcega and immured in a tavern in Almeria, and there she remained, calling herself mine until for her sake I had hamstrung Mingalarios, the Chief Magistrate of Estepa.

VALIANO: The Devil take you!

VALLEJO: And I cut off Vicente Aremoso's right arm, fighting man to man in the Percheles of Malaga, with the water up to our chests.

VALIANO: Be silent, Vallejo. Continue, Leonardo, for if your sister is as beautiful as you paint her, she may advance your fortunes beyond all your expectations.

LEONARDO: Senor, your hands ply me unceasingly with bounties beyond number. But as to my sister, believe me, she surpasses everything I have said of her.

VALLEJO: Our Lady of Pilar de Zaragoza bless me! Oh, thieves, thieves! Leonardo, to arms, to arms!

LEONARDO: What is it? What have you seen?

VALIANO: Who's there?

VALLEJO: Hold, hold, senor, do not lift a finger: they've already fled, every one of them. Ah, sucklings! Do you scramble pell-mell to escape me? You can be grateful . . .

VALIANO: To whom?

VALLEJO: That's my own secret. Senor Leonardo, when we have seen our master to his house, let us undertake a reconnaissance, you and I, to Bulbeja's tavern.

LEONARDO: What for?

VALLEJO: To ferret out these barbarians who just went past here; for according to my informations they arrived not half an hour since from Marbella and have in their clutches a maiden like a seraphim.

VALIANO: What's the fellow talking about, Leonardo?

LEONARDO: I don't understand him, senor.

VALLEJO: Don't understand me? Do you think I discourse gibberish? We'll see since when they dare turn out a cow to pasture without registering it first with the trap-keeper.

VALIANO: Leonardo, if you are willing, I should like to mention this matter to some of the elders of my household, so that they'll not be able to say that in such an affair I did not take them into my confidence.

LEONARDO: As you wish, senor.

VALLEJO: Let us go, senor, for I've certain duties at hand which I must attend to before daybreak.

VALIANO: What duties, you sot?

VALLEJO: Senor, a matter filled with jewels of honor.

VALIANO: What sort of jewelry?

VALLEJO: I've already told Senor Leonardo: I must recover certain monies from certain ruffians who've come here to mischief the place; we'll see who gave them their licence without their first registering before this boot.

VALIANO: Good Lord, enough; go.

VALLEJO: God forbid it; for your person is safer in my ward and shadow than if you were locked in the Keep of Medina, having heaved tight after you that ponderous drawbridge behind which the army of night is secured.

V

EUFEMIA: Cristina, how do you account for this long oblivion to which my dear brother, Leonardo, has consigned me without a word; for it's been days and days since I've had a letter from him. Oh blessed souls in Purgatory, direct my brother's heart so that either letters from him or he himself may come to give me joy and delight.

CRISTINA: Hush, my lady, don't weary yourself; I'm sure he hasn't been able to, especially since no man who serves someone else is often his own master. I'd swear it's not that he hasn't meant to; but no doubt his lord's more arduous affairs prevent him from doing what he'd like to. So don't fret, my lady, for when you least expect it, your wishes will be granted.

EUFEMIA: Ah, my friend, may God in His vast mercy favor us with letters from my brother and so fill our house with happiness and contentment.

GIPSY: Peace be unto this house; peace be unto this house! God save you, worshipful lady, God save you; give me a little alms, lady with the face of gold, face of an eternal bride. Give me some little thing, and may God prosper you and give you all you desire, lady with the kind face, kind face.

CRISTINA: Can't you stand out there and ask for it? Oh, my lady, the impertinence of some people! Instead of making you take pity on them and their poverty, it brings you to hate their barefaced pestering.

GIPSY: Hush, hush, pretty lady, pretty lady; give me a little money in God's name, and he'll send you blessings; what would you wish for, you and the lady?

EUFEMIA: I? Oh, misery! What good fortune could I hope for, who have had no mother since my mother bore me?

GIPSY: Hush, hush, worshipful lady. Put a little coin here; you'll learn wonders.

EUFEMIA: What have I to learn, I who for so long have been as empty of all consolation as I have been filled to overflowing with anxieties, miseries, and vexations of spirit?

CRISTINA: Oh, my lady, if you give her something we'll hear the same gibble-gabble that her sort peddles to everybody.

GIPSY: Listen to me, listen, you beak for a magpie; we know more things when we want to than anybody will believe.

EUFEMIA: Enough; here, give her this with God's blessing.

CRISTINA: Make her tell your fortune before she goes, in good faith.

EUFEMIA: Let her go, and God be with her; I'm not in the mood today for such whimsies.

GIPSY: Gently, gently, kind lady; don't wear yourself out before your time, for you're heavy-burdened.

EUFEMIA: Indeed I am; you were right that time.

CRISTINA: Don't be sad, my lady; jokes and lies, that's all her sort ever spew out of their mouths.

GIPSY: And the basket of face-paints you keep hidden in the barley-cupboard; is that a joke?

CRISTINA: Oh, my lady, and she uses the Devil's mouth to talk out of! Or else may the mother that bore me have a bad hundred years in Purgatory; and she told more truth than anyone in the world.

EUFEMIA: But is it possible? It is true about the face-paints?

CRISTINA: As surely as we're standing here. Tell me more, woman.

GIPSY: I'd not want to make you blush, what with your mistress right here.

CRISTINA: And you won't, either, by the life of my soul. What could you possibly tell that would cast aspersions on my honor?

GIPSY: Will you let me say?

CRISTINA: Tell away, and there an end to it.

GIPSY: The pair of turtledoves, which you gave your mistress to understand the cats ate, where were they eaten?

CRISTINA: Look at the things she rakes up! That was even before my Lord Leonardo went away.

GIPSY: True, true; but you and the stableboy ate them under the landing of the stairs. Oh, you know it's the truth I'm telling!

CRISTINA: And I'd rather the earth swallowed me up before I'm due, than stay as I am and hear you tell any bigger truths.

GIPSY: My lady, there is someone far away from here who loves you dearly, and although at this moment he is high in his master's favor, before long his life will be in danger, because of a treacherous plot that's hatching; but there, rest easy, for though all this will come about because of you, yet God who is the true judge and suffers no falsehood to remain hidden for long, will reveal the truth at last.

EUFEMIA: Oh, miserable woman! Did you say it was because of me that this person will be in danger? And who could it be, wretch, but my beloved brother?

GIPSY: Lady, I know no more; but you saw that the things I told your servant were no lies. I'm going; good fortune attend you; and if I learn anything more I'll come back and tell you. God keep you.

CRISTINA: And what of me? Won't you tell me anything? Will I marry or stay spinster?

GIPSY: You'll be wife to nine husbands and all of them living. What more do you want to know? God console you, lady.

EUFEMIA: Won't you tell me any more about this that concerns me? Will you leave me uncertain as to what will become of me?

GIPSY: I don't know anything more to tell you, except that your fate will never be so hard, even in the time of greatest peril, as to make either prudence or fortune forsake you; and that in the end you will all be as happy and contented as the Divine Mercy can make you.

CRISTINA: Oh, the bitterness for me to bear, my lady! Did you hear her say that I'd be wife to nine husbands, nine, and all of them living? Oh, the sad fate that awaits me! And how could that be possible?

EUFEMIA: Be still. Leave me. For although everything that these creatures say is, we are told, patently false, still what she told me has left me more sorrowful and afflicted than the dark night. Let us go in.

VI

VALIANO: Can it be possible, Pedro? Did you in truth stay in the house of this same Eufemia, the sister of this wicked and treacherous Leonardo, whom I set in so exalted a position?

PEDRO: Yes, senor, I did.

VALIANO: And you, you yourself, slept with her in her own bed?

PEDRO: And I myself slept with her in her own bed; what more do you want?

VALIANO: It remains for you to tell me, my most faithful Pedro, of the delights you enjoyed with her.

PEDRO: Senor, I enjoyed the same with her as I enjoy with all the others. I hadn't taken more than a very few turns in the street, with an occasional glance at the window, believe me, when she singled me out and sent after me a slip of a servant she keeps by her, called, for convenience, Cristina.

VALIANO: And what did the servant say to you?

PEDRO: She asked whether I had need of anything in their house. I, as I'd realized before this and told Your Worship, knew that there'd be no great need for match-makers, and I went in for a nibble, especially since the lady knew me from before and had taken my money more than once. I was a guest there that night, and three others after that; and since by then I'd memorized all the points of her person, as I'd promised you I would, my lord, I came to give you a report on what had happened.

VALIANO: And what had?

PEDRO: What had happened was that she gave me, to wear in my hat or bonnet, a piece of a hair from a large mole on her left shoulder; and, knowing this to be an undeniable token with which to confront her brother and your protégé, the Lord Leonardo, I decided to fetch it back to you, and here it is. So now I've done my duty in a way which does justice both to what I am, and to the loyalty which I owe you as your vassal. And you, my lord, have made certain that no traitor can mock at you, nor—and he your servant too—challenge you to such a thing, and above all when so great a prize of honor hung in the balance.

VALIANO: Have no doubt, Pedro, but that I am aware that this traitor, under the guise of exemplary service to me, had designed to smirch the honor of this ancient house; but I promise you that he will pay for this treachery with nothing less than his life, and that you at the same time will be recompensed with copious favors for your own exemplary services.

PEDRO: That's as it should be, senor; let the traitor be exposed as what he is, and the honest and loyal servant remunerated for his fidelity.

VALIANO: Let us go, Pedro, for I promise you this punishment will be a warning both for those who are present and those who are to come.

PEDRO: I am coming, senor, and may justice fall on all traitors.

VII

EUFEMIA: Oh, Cristina, sister, come and give me your advice as to what I should do, for my afflicted heart is compassed about by cruel anguish and forebodings. What can I say, but that ever since that gipsy was here I have not lived a single hour without suffering a thousand qualms and tremors, for even though I realized that her words were nonsense, I read her disheartening prognostications in her eyes.

CRISTINA: Oh, no such thing, senora. Oh, in God's name don't imagine misfortunes and present me with such a face of sadness; because for every once they hit, and that by hazard, on the truth, they go wide of the mark two thousand times; for all their talk is only a way of fishing here and there for whatever they can find. And since that's their calling, senora, don't you see that it's impossible for any person of sense to give them the least credence in the world?

EUFEMIA: Oh, Cristina! I understand that it's all just as you say, but what am I to do if I cannot rid my imagination of these things?

CRISTINA: Calm yourself, senora; leave it in the hands of God Who is the amender of all things. But by my mother's ghost, here is Melchior Ortiz. Ah, brother Melchior, you are welcome. What news have you brought for my mistress? How is my lord?

MELCHIOR: He's well, though they haven't done to him what they said they were going to.

EUFEMIA: What were they going to do to him? Tell me at once.

MELCHIOR: God preserve me! Don't be downhearted, senora, for I know for a fact that first of all they'll give him confession, because one of those fellows who go about with hoods on, said so.

CRISTINA: Hoods? You mean friars?

MELCHIOR: That's it.

CRISTINA: What did they tell you, Melchior?

MELCHIOR: That he must put his soul in order, and then there'd be nothing more for them to do, please God, except when his head's lopped from his shoulders they'll carry him out of the dungeon.

EUFEMIA: Oh, Cristina! I'm killed!

CRISTINA: There, there, senora, don't say such a thing. Can't you see that he's raving, more than likely? Didn't my lord say anything to you? Did he give you a letter for the senora?

MELCHIOR: He told me to come back here and stay, because he wouldn't be wanting anyone to wait on him once he was dead.

CRISTINA: Dead? What are you saying?

MELCHIOR: I'm saying that it wasn't his idea that they should kill him; he'd have gone on just as he was, with his windpipe and all; but everyone must go his own way.

CRISTINA: Donkey! Did he give you a letter?

MELCHIOR: Do you hear that? "Donkey," to a man who can pronounce on every vineyard and almost farm for miles about!

CRISTINA: Have you brought a letter from my lord? Just tell me that.

MELCHIOR: Haven't I already said yes? What devils possess you?

CRISTINA: Well, where is it?

MELCHIOR: Come now, Cristina, wash my feet and perfume my head and set a meal before me, and no more of your contrariness.

CRISTINA: I wash you? The fires of Hell wash you into a cinder. Give me the letter. Where have you put it?

MELCHIOR: Look for it in this sack, senora.

CRISTINA: I can't find anything in here.

MELCHIOR: Well, if you can't, what do you want me to do? Do you expect me to remember where it is?

EUFEMIA: Oh, give it to me; or in the name of the only God tell me where you put it.

MELCHIOR: Senora, let me go back and see if I can catch my master before he dies, and ask him where I put it, and there an end to it.

EUFEMIA: Oh, misery; what is that bit of white sticking out of the lining of your cloak?

MELCHIOR: Don't touch it, in the Devil's name; it's a piece of inky paper my master gave me for the senora.

EUFEMIA: Oh, sinner that I am before God! What do you think we've been begging you for these two hours past?

MELCHIOR: What? Is this a letter? And there, I took it for a paper. Take it; it has only itself to blame if it didn't fall out on the way here. For I've no more remembered it since he who, God willing, will be snuffed out sometime this next week, put it there, than I have the first bowl of pap my mother ever set before me.

EUFEMIA: Sister Cristina, you read it to me, for I've not the strength even to look at it.

CRISTINA: "Let this be given into the hands of the cruellest and most wicked she the world until now has seen."

MELCHIOR: Oh, according to the address, it's for you, Cristina.

CRISTINA: Hold your tongue.

Letter from Leonardo to Eufemia

"If God, Eufemia, according to the account of just complaints I am bound to render to Him concerning your unjust and abominable person, were to administer to you your just reward, I cannot think but that your corrupt and infernal body would be unable to support what for its foul and unspeakable deeds it deserves. What cause, accursed sister, could bring you—you, born of such parents and descended from forebearers so illustrious (whose own virtues, had you been dutiful, had prevailed with you in everything)—what cause could bring you to embrace such dissolution and depravity that you not only offer yourself freely to any who lust after your infamous body, but even give such part of it to your lovers that they, publicly and in the rubric of justice, can display mole hairs from your person to confound me? As for me, learn for a certainty that I shall die for having praised one of whom I was ignorant; for the sentence of that lord whom I intended to betray through you cannot be revoked, and I have been granted no more than twenty days in which to set my soul at peace and discharge all things outstanding. And since uttering complaints to you would be to waste my words on the wind, live as you please, false and defiled woman, for I in my innocence shall pay with my head for what you committed in your depravity."

EUFEMIA: What is this? What do I hear? Oh, miserable creature that I am! What vast impurities have I practiced? And who is he who can, truthfully and without the greatest treachery and deceit, display tokens from my person, or even so much as claim to have seen me through a thousand walls? Cristina, you can bear me witness.

CRISTINA: Ah, senora! Whatever anguish my lord has suffered, I have been the cause, and not you. And if you will forgive me, I will tell you of my part in this matter.

EUFEMIA: Say what you please, and be certain of pardon if you can at all enlighten me concerning what I have heard in this heart-stricken letter.

CRISTINA: Know then, senora, that though I confess my error to you, it was through ignorance that I committed it, and therefore my sin is not so great as if I had done it from malice.

EUFEMIA: Tell me and be done with it; it's not the time now to stand wasting words; tell me what it is and don't keep me in mid-air, for I'm dying until I hear it.

CRISTINA: Know, then, my lady, that several days ago there was a man, not from these parts I thought, who came inquiring for you, and asked me whether he might see you or talk with you. I told him I was certain that would be impossible because of the strictness of your virtuous retirement; but he so importuned me that in the end I described to him all the marks of your body; and not content with this, he begged me to cut off a piece of the hair which grows on the mole on your right shoulder. I never imagined that such a thing could imperil your honor or be of any use to anybody, so when I saw he was so desperate I took it from you while you were asleep and gave it to him.

EUFEMIA: Say no more; for some great calamity seems to have befallen because of it. Let us go, for I am determined now to launch myself upon something which all my life I have thought of doing. Within the course of these twenty days I shall go there, in as clandestine and disguised a manner as may be, and we shall see whether I cannot somewhat ease the life of this dearly beloved brother who, without knowing the truth, has written me so many insults and so many pitiable complaints.

CRISTINA: Do that, and waste no time by the way, and I would lay my life on it that with God's help all will be saved. Let us go.

MELCHIOR: Do I have to come, too?

CHRISTINA: Yes, brother; who's to see to our comforts on the way, if not you?

MELCHIOR: God help me, a man might be using it to learn mapmaking for mariners, and not have to repeat himself on this road as often. Well, oh well.

VIII

PEDRO: Oh, it prospers with me, it does; as my name's Pedro and didn't I know where to seize an advantage? Oh, the astuteness with which I tripped up that upstart, Leonardo! Oh, how happy fortune has made me, and think of the credit I've gained with Valiano! Excellent; and not many days now till the period of procrastination is up, that they gave him to settle his affairs outstanding, if he had any. And then they'll wreak justice upon him, and with that stroke what man in all this country will be so favored by fortune as I? But, might the lackey, Vallejo, bring witness against me? No, for the sum of two doubloons which I promised him on the road as he came with me, he said he'd destroy any, though they came in their multitudes, who might give the lie to my story. But I must go; who is this coming? I'd not be overheard by anyone till all risks are run and the thing done.

IX

POLO: Oh, God be praised for letting me get out from under the nose of that importunate Valiano, my master, at least for a moment. He doesn't seem to do anything all day long but think of things which have nothing to do with anything. Now what amazes me is that Leonardo, who everyone took to be so honorable and prudent a young man, should attempt to deceive my master by giving him to understand that his sister was so virtuous that she was in every way worthy to be my lord's wife. Well, as he baked he must eat, for it won't be long before his throat will be paying for the sins of his tongue. God keep me out of it. And let me follow my own planet, this way; for if the woman, Eulallia, my love, will comply with me as she's promised me, I shall be one of the men most pampered by fortune in all my genealogy. Here I am at her door. I know she sleeps in this chamber here, over the street. Now what signals shall I make so that she may appear? Oh, luck's with me: that's she who's singing.

NEGRESS *(sings)*: Gila Gonzale
from the village calls:
Mothers, I can no say
will I open to him.
Gila Gonzale
to the tower calls
open to me your voice
daughter Leonora
because the horse
he wet my little cannon.
Mothers, I can no say
will I open to him.

POLO: Ah, my love, my lady, Eulallia! Ah, senora! How intox-
icated she is in her music!

EULALLIA: Jesu! The God Almighty expose me, creator of heaven
and the earths!

POLO: Ah, Senora Eulallia, do not blench, do not tremble, for he
who calls you desires nothing but to serve you in every way.

EULALLIA: You suppose that it is good examples at the window
of one retired honorable dame such like I am, the doing such
courtesies at such an hour?

POLO: She mustn't have recognized me. Ah, Senora Eulallia!

EULALLIA: Bad times come and catch you! You imagine it is nice
at one daughter of she honest man the make some rude wig-
wags a whore would insult with?

POLO: Oh, sinner that I am! Show yourself, Eulallia, at this window, and look at me, and see for yourself who I am.

EULALLIA: Who is under there? Jesu! Whether the voice lies it at
me, or else those is my Lord Pollos who is calling.

POLO: Oh, blessed is whatever made it plain to you!

EULALLIA: Oh, my lords, at such an hour!

POLO: My lady, for the serving of such a piece and morsel as your
worship is, it is still early.

EULALLIA: But more truer, I could not very much dispose.

POLO: God preserve you. And why not?

EULALLIA: For my lord that one cousin I have like a big lady
which an objects of lye gave to me for make yellow my hairs;
but for since I am like too delicate, so it chewed my head
down to like one sponge; I think we could not very much
dispose.

POLO: God save me! And is there nothing can be done for it?

EULALLIA: Yes, yes, God reserve me! For I was send me visit at
that lady Abbot that is nuns with Saint Paula, which told

me she would send me one liquids by which will take it off from me like hands.

POLO: But have you become a blonde now?

EULALLIA: Certainly. Because am I not have hairs like the other?

POLO: Indeed, your hair. Even now, in my eyes, there is no brocade can compare with it.

EULALLIA: But by my faith, during five nights I was doing prayers to Senor Nicholas from Tramentinos.

POLO: Saint Nicholas of Tolentino? Why did you pray to him, my lady?

EULALLIA: I want to marrying on to my masters, and so God would supply me one husband to my contentments.

POLO: Away with you, senora; how can you consider such a thing? Didn't you promise to marry me?

EULALLIA: How, senor; can you see no more farther than that? You suppose I was show that way good examples and account for my ancestrals? What would tell you how much lords she is I have loving me in this countries?

POLO: And the promise, senora, that you made me?

EULALLIA: Senor, where she must go the rights are lost; and the honor could not be in one sack with fallows.

POLO: But what dishonors could you lose, senora, by marrying me?

EULALLIA: I could see it already now, senor; you more want to rapture me and then lost me in countries that I know you.

POLO: My Queen, can you say such a thing, and to me? For I would forsake you long before I forsook my life.

EULALLIA: Oh, deceivinger! Oh, that one twisting sickness did scramble up each mans! Drop that dog some difference bone, because I am already retired of her.

POLO: Truly, senora, I think you must be mistaken. But tell me, who is it you wish to marry?

EULALLIA: I wants with one dung-king-driver; my master say no, that he more rather with one pothecaries; I says him no; he say, "Be quite, girl, since which has office enjoys malpractice."

POLO: And am I not an official?

EULALLIA: Which fishes, Senor Pollos?

POLO: Skin curer, cloak holder, spindle and distaff whittler, bottom-stopper and mouth-maker for wine-gourds, and a thousand other offices, by means of which, though you see me now serving as a lackey, I shall be able to maintain you in every way as befits your honor. Only when you come, don't fail to bring along enough for the first day's expenses, and after that I will make you mistress of a great hall and a canopied bed in tooled leather. What more could you ask for, my lady?

EULALLIA: Yes, now that is content me. But do you know what I would wishing, Senor Pollos?

POLO: Not until you tell me.

EULALLIA: For you buy me one lady-monkeys, and one parrots.

POLO: What for, senora?

EULALLIA: The parrot for teach him speaking at in a cage, and she monkeys for have him at my doors and be mistress of my hole.

POLO: You mean your hall.

EULALLIA: Yes, yes already I tell you, to have in my hole; but you know you must beseech with Senora Dona Betriz for bore me one fans for the journeys.

POLO: Why will you need a fan, senora?

EULALLIA: For the front to my face, because if somebodies that is known he would not knew me.

POLO: Senora, I will do it; but I must go now, because the whole country will be turning out to see that poor Leonardo, on whom they're to execute justice this very day.

EULALLIA: Ay, miserableness Truly, it turn me so sad like he is my own son; but if you want for one oceans you end with dancing.

POLO: Farewell, my lady, for it is already almost full day, and people will be up earlier than usual this morning to get there in time to find good places. Because even though he wasn't from these parts, he was so beloved by them all, poor boy, that everybody will be there to strengthen him with their prayers.

EULALLIA: Ay! Such bitter for the mother which bore him.

POLO: Even my master, Valiano, grieves inwardly to think of his death; but that Pedro, his rival, the one who brought the evidence from his sister, accuses him as stubbornly as ever, and it's that that's brought him to the fix he's in. God be with you.

EULALLIA: Hooly spirits preserve you my life and soul, and delivering you meantimes.

POLO: A millstone mash the likes of her! I've decided to sell her in the first place we come to, saying that she's my slave; the airs she gives herself! I'm amazed she didn't ask for a canopy and all to drape her buttocks with. And me without a farthing; maybe she thinks she can conjure coins from between my ribs, insisting on a parrot and a monkey!

EULALLIA: Senor Pollos, Senor Pollos!

POLO: What is it, my life?

EULALLIA: Fetching me for tomorrows one small bit of mustard with little of serpentine like they calling of the bitches.

POLO: Pitch turpentine? What do you want that for, senora?

EULALLIA: To making one pleach for the hands.

POLO: Oh senora, I am content with the color you are; there's no need for you to tamper with it.

EULALLIA: So is truth, for but my faces is browns, the body he has like twice velvet.

POLO: If you were the least bit whiter, you'd be worthless. Farewell. I love you as you are, and you'll fetch more money that way.

EULALLIA: Guide you the same bawd which led one loving shebulls.

X

CRISTINA: This is a good place, now, senora, for you can wait here until Valiano comes and then say what you like to him.

EUFEMIA: May that Almighty Lord who knows and understands all things divulge so foul a treachery and force it into the light, so that the truth may be plain and my beloved brother freed, since both he and I are innocent of what we are so falsely charged with.

CRISTINA: Be patient, senora, for the time has come when the truth will be discovered, and then let everyone be spoken of as he deserves.

EUFEMIA: Listen; footsteps approaching. Here they come; and that one on the right, I would say by his bearing, must be Valiano, lord of all this country round about.

CRISTINA: Oh, my lady! And that one who is with him is the same stranger who importuned me until I described you to him, with all the marks of your body.

EUFEMIA: Hush, they're talking as they come.

VALIANO: Tell me, Pedro, is everything ready?

PEDRO: Yes, my lord; I have arranged it with all possible care so that the traitor may receive his due, and your mind be set at rest.

VALIANO: You have done well. Who are these people?

PEDRO: I do not recognize them, my lord. They must be strangers to these parts.

VALIANO: I should think so; what grace and bearing that first one has! You are welcome, senora, to dine with me at my table.

EUFEMIA: Illustrious senor, I am indeed a stranger here; and since you are the lord of this place, I crave justice of you.

VALIANO: I am delighted infinitely to discover that I have it in my power to do you whatever favor; for though I owe as much to any lady who is a stranger here, beyond that your manner and presence would compel anyone to enter completely into your service; therefore demand what you will, and as for the justice you crave, it will not in the smallest detail be denied you.

EUFEMIA: It will be justice, senor, for I have been foully wronged.

VALIANO: Wronged? And in my domain? I will not let such a thing go unpunished.

VALLEJO: By Jesus, senor! Let us assemble the whole household, and put me at the head of them, and you'll see how quickly I'll turn the whole city out by the ears, and not a finger raised in resistance, either.

VALIANO: Hold your tongue, Vallejo. Tell me, senora; who was it that wronged you?

EUFEMIA: My lord, that traitor standing there beside you.

PEDRO: I? Senora, are you mocking me, or making up some game?

EUFEMIA: Neither, deceitful! How many nights did you sleep with me in my bed; but the last night of all you stole from me a jewel of great value that was under the bolster.

PEDRO: What are you saying, senora? You must have mistaken me for someone else, for I neither recognize you nor have the least notion who you are. How can you accuse me of a thing that I never in all my life could have even considered doing?

EUFEMIA: Oh, liar! Was it not enough to make use of my body as you made use of it; did you have to go so far as to steal what belonged to me?

VALIANO: Pedro, answer; is what this lady says true?

PEDRO: My answer, senor, is that it is the wildest imputation in the world; I not only do not know her, I never saw her before in all my life.

EUFEMIA: Oh, senor, this traitor denies it only so that he can trick me out of my jewel.

PEDRO: Call neither me nor anyone else "traitor," since if there is any treachery about you are its author, accusing someone who never in his life set eyes on you.

EUFEMIA: Oh, liar! You? Never slept with me?

PEDRO: I tell you I neither know you nor have the least notion who you are.

EUFEMIA: Oh, my lord, make him swear an oath on that; that will force the truth out of him.

VALIANO: Lay your hand on your sword, Pedro.

PEDRO: I swear, my lord, by everything a man can swear by, that I neither slept with her, nor have ever seen the inside of her house, nor recognize her, nor know what she is talking about.

EUFEMIA: In that case, of walking treachery, let your ears note carefully what your infernal tongue has spoken, for you have condemned yourself out of your own mouth.

PEDRO: How? What are you saying? Now what are you claiming against me?

EUFEMIA: Tell me, wretch; if you do not recognize me, how is it that you have managed to level accusations at me and bear so false a witness against me?

PEDRO: I? Witness? The women is mad!

EUFEMIA: I? Mad? Did you not declare that you had slept with me?

PEDRO: I, say such a thing? Senor, if ever I did, may I be most justly condemned to death, and in your presence meet an ignominious end at the hands of the common hangman.

EUFEMIA: So, so, perfidious; and if you never slept with me, how does there come to be such a scandal in these parts, all spread from your testimony and the accusation which you, who do not so much as recognize me, levelled against me?

PEDRO: Get out of here with your testimony, or your gibberish!

EUFEMIA: Tell me, you who respect no law, have you not stated that you slept with Leonardo's sister?

PEDRO: Indeed I have; and brought tokens besides from her very body.

EUFEMIA: And those tokens, how did you come by them? Oh, fabric of treacheries, I who am standing here before you am Leonardo's sister; how is it that you do not recognize me, since you have slept with me so often?

VALIANO: Some vast deceit is disclosed here, or I am mistaken.

CRISTINA: You spittle in the face of justice, can you deny that you pestered me to give you those same tokens of my lady's, though now in my disguise you do not recognize me? And when I saw you were so desperate, I cut off a piece of hair from a mole she has on her right shoulder and gave it to you, never suspecting that that could do anybody any harm.

VALIANO: Ah liar, you cannot deny the truth of this, for with your own mouth you confessed it.

VALLEJO: Away with your buzzing, blow-fly of Arjona! This Pedro would have implicated me as well in his villainy.

VALIANO: How is that?

VALLEJO: He begged me, on the road as we were going, to testify along with him as to how he had slept with Leonardo's sister, and for that he promised me the price of a pair of shoes, and I should have been sad to have got a hundred strokes of the lash instead of a pair of shoes.

VALIANO: Sweet Christ! Take this traitor and lay him on the torments of Talion; for I was convinced of the virtue of my faithful Leonardo. Lead him out of prison and restore him to his rank, and then cut off this traitor's head on the block that was laid for my dear Leonardo.

VALLEJO: Quite so, my lord, just as you say.

VALIANO: And for this noble lady who with such astuteness contrived to save her brother's life, let her remain in our lands and be their ruler and my wife, for even so I cannot repay her for the tribulations which her brother suffered in prison, and she in saving him.

VALLEJO: Senor, that same fountain of false witness and accusations, the miserable Pedro, is now as impounded as any treasure; I delivered him into the hands of the jailor with those same compliments you said.

VALIANO: Now, by heaven, let new liveries be cut for every servant in my house; and you, my lady, give me your hand and let us go in and eat, for I desire both you and your brother to dine with me to rejoice at so happy an event; and then let us be married, as I promised Leonardo at the beginning.

EUFEMIA: My lord, my happiness shall be all in obeying you.

VALLEJO: And there goes my master, arm in arm with the girl; but I've got out of this affair better than any, a hundred strokes for false witness. I'm going; they'll be needing me in the house. Friends, take care to do nothing but eat and walk about the square, and you'll see a traitor beheaded and an honest man who in the untangling of this plot has shown himself to be prudent, wise, and diligent, freed and rewarded.

Et vale

The Life of Lazarillo de Tormes
His Fortunes and Adversities

For the present translation I have used the Alcalá edition of 1554. W.S.M.

Author's Prologue

It is only right, to my mind, that things so remarkable, which happen to have remained unheard and unseen until now, should be brought to the attention of many and not lie buried in the sepulcher of oblivion. The reader may find matter here to entertain him, and even he who does no more than dip into this book will have his reward in pleasure. For this reason Pliny remarks that there is no book however bad which does not have some good in it. Especially as all tastes are not the same, and what one man will not eat another man pines for. Thus we see the same objects scorned by some and not by others. And therefore nothing of this sort should be destroyed or thrown away unless it is utterly detestable, but on the contrary such things should be brought to the knowledge of everyone, especially if they are utterly harmless and even likely to bear some fruit.

If it were otherwise, there are very few who would write just for one reader, because it is hard work, and those who undertake it hope to be rewarded, not in money, but in having the efforts seen and read and, when possible, praised. That is why Cicero says: "Honor is the nurse of the arts."

Does anyone suppose that the soldier who is first on the scaling ladder is there because his life is abhorrent to him? Certainly not. It is the desire for praise which leads him to run such risks. And it is the same with the arts and the art of letters. Take for example a theological student who is a candidate for a degree. He preaches an excellent sermon and indeed his concern for the cure of souls is fervent and genuine, but ask him politely whether he is offended when they say to him: "Oh Your Reverence, that was wonderful!" Or consider the knight Don Fulano whose jousting was disastrous and who gave his coat of mail to the buffoon who praised his skill with the lance. What would he have given if the clown had told the truth?

It is the same way with everything. I confess that I am no more saintly than my neighbors and so it would not be a matter of indifference to me if this trifle, written in my crude style, were to entertain and delight all who were drawn to it, giving them a glimpse of one man's life among so many shifting fortunes, dangers, and adversities.

I beseech Your Excellency to accept the humble handiwork of one who would be richer if his ability were equal to his desire. And since Your Excellency has written to ask for a full account of this subject I thought best not to begin in the middle but at the beginning, so as to present a complete narrative of myself. At the same time my history may lead those who have inherited noble estates to consider how little credit is due to them, since Fortune was partial to them in the first place, and how much more they have accomplished who have had Fortune against them from the start, and who have nothing to thank but their own labor and skill at the oars for bringing them into a safe harbor.

Lazaro Recounts His Life and Tells of His Parents

Well in the first place Your Excellency should know that they call me Lazaro de Tormes, and I am the son of Tome Gonzalez and of Antona Perez, both of them natives of Tejares, a hamlet in the neighborhood of Salamanca. I was born in the Tormes river, which is why I took the surname I bear. The way of it was this. My father, God rest his soul, had the job of tending a grist mill on the bank of that river; he was a miller there for over fifteen years. And one night when my mother was pregnant with me she was in the mill and the labor pains came on and she gave birth to me right there. So that I can truly claim to have been born in the river.

Then when I was eight years old some people who had come to have their grain milled discovered a number of ragged and bleeding wounds in their sacks, and the cause of these was imputed to my father. As a result he was arrested, and he confessed and did not deny it, and he suffered persecution for the sake of justice. I hope to God that he is in glory, for the scripture says that all those who are there are blessed. At that time an expedition was being got up against the Moors. My father, who was currently away from home as a result of the aforementioned disaster, went along as a gentleman's groom, and like a loyal servant, perished at his master's side.

My widowed mother, finding herself without husband or protection, decided to cleave unto the good and become one of them, so she came to the city and rented a little house and set about cooking for a number of the students. She also did laundry for some of the Knight Commander of Magdalena's stable-boys, and thus it was that she came to frequent the stables.

She and a dark complexioned groom there got to know each other and sometimes he would come to our house and leave in the morning. Other times he would appear at the door in the daytime pretending that he wanted to buy eggs, and get into the house that way. When he first started coming to the house I didn't like him, and his black color and his ugly face frightened me. But then when I saw that we ate better as a result of his visits I got to like him very much, because he always brought bread with him, and pieces of meat, and wood in the winter to keep us warm.

These visits and conversations continued, and as a result my mother presented me one day with a pretty little pickaninny whom I jogged in my arms and helped to keep warm.

And I remember once when my black stepfather was playing with the little boy, the child noticed that my mother and I were white and my stepfather was not, and he was frightened and ran away from my mother, and pointing a finger at his father, said, "Mother, bogey-man!"

My stepfather laughed and said, "Son of a bitch!"

I was very small at the time but I was struck by what my little brother had said, and I thought, "How many there must be in the world who run away from others because they do not see themselves!"

As our luck would have it, Zaide's comings and goings (for that was his name) were mentioned to the head steward, who looked into the matter and discovered that my stepfather had been helping himself to about half of the barley which was provided for the horses, and had kept pretending that bran, wood, currycombs, cloths, horse-blankets and saddle-blankets had been lost, and that when nothing else was left he had taken the shoes off the horses' feet and had brought the proceeds from all these things to my mother, to help bring up my little brother. We should not be surprised at a priest or a friar if the one robs the poor and the other steals from his order so as to provide for the ladies of his flock and for other members of his calling, when love led a poor slave to do a thing like this.

And all that I've mentioned was proved against him, and more besides, due to the fact that they questioned me and threatened me if I did not tell, and since I was only a child I answered them and told them everything that I knew, even to a number of horse-shoes which, at my mother's bidding, I had sold to a blacksmith.

They flogged my poor stepfather and flung boiling oil over him, and my mother was sentenced, for the sake of justice, to the hundred lashes which are customary in such cases, and she was forbidden besides ever to set foot again in the house of the aforementioned Commander, or to admit the luckless Zaide into hers.

Rather than throw the rope after the bucket, the poor woman got a grip on herself and obeyed the sentence. And in order to get out of harm's way and escape malicious talk, she went to work as a servant to the people who at that time were living in the Solana inn. There she was subjected to a thousand indignities, but she managed to bring up my little brother until he could walk, and me until I was big enough to fetch wine to the lodgers, and candles, and anything else they sent me for.

At that time a blind man came to stay at the inn and took a notion that I would do as a guide for him. He asked my mother to give me to him, which she did, telling him that I was the son of a good man who had died for the glory of the faith at the battle of Los Gelves, and that she hoped to God that I would not turn out to be any worse than my father. And she begged him to be kind to me and look after me, since I was an orphan.

He said that he would, and that with him I would be not a servant but a son. And so I began serving and guiding my new old master.

When we had been in Salamanca for several days my master grew dissatisfied with his takings and decided to go somewhere else. When we were ready to leave I went to see my mother. Both of us cried, and she gave me her blessing.

"Son," she said, "I know that I will never see you again. Try to be good, and may God be your guide. I have brought you up and settled you with a good master. Look after yourself."

Then I went back to my master, who was waiting for me.

We left Salamanca and got to the bridge. At one end of it there is a stone animal which is something like a bull. The blind man told me to go over near it and when I was there he said, "Put your ear to the bull, Lazaro, and you'll hear a loud noise inside it."

I was simple enough to believe him, and when he could feel that my head was up close to the stone he shot up his hand and gave my head such a mighty whack against that infernal bull that I suffered from the goring for three days afterwards, and he said to me, "Stupid! Get it through your head: a blind man's boy has to keep one jump ahead of the devil himself."

And he had a good laugh at his own joke.

It seemed to me that at that moment I awoke out of the simplicity in which I had remained like a sleeping child. And I said to myself, "He's right. I'd better keep my eyes open and my wits about me, for I'm on my own, and I'll have to figure out how to manage for myself."

We started out on our way and in a few days he had taught me the thieves' jargon. And when he saw that I was a bright boy he was very pleased, and he said, "Silver and gold have I none, but I can give you plenty of good tips on how to get along."

And it was true. For after God it was he who gave me life, and though he was blind himself he lighted up things for me and guided me along in the way of the world.

It is a joy to me to recount these childish matters to Your Excellency, to show how much virtue there can be in those who are born to low estate and drag themselves up, and how much vice in the great who let themselves be dragged down.

Well, to get back to my good master the blind man, and his affairs, let me assure Your Excellency that since God created the world He never made a shrewder or wiser man. He was an eagle at the business. He knew well over a hundred prayers by heart. He had a low-pitched, relaxed, and extremely sonorous voice which made the whole church resound when he prayed. At such times his face was humble and devout and he would conduct himself with extreme propriety, not waving his hands and making faces as some people do when they pray, rolling their eyes and screwing up their mouths.

Besides this he knew a thousand other ways and means of extracting money. He gave out that he knew prayers for all sorts of particular purposes: for women who could not conceive, for those who were in labor, for those who were unhappily married and wanted their husbands to love them. He would look into the future for pregnant mothers and tell them whether it was a boy or a girl.

As for medicine, he said that Galen never knew the half of what he did when it came to toothache, fainting fits, and women's troubles. In fact no matter what the ailment might be, nobody ever came to him but he'd tell them: "Do this or that, go and pick such-and-such an herb, or such-and-such a root."

The result was that he had an enormous following, especially among the women, who believed every word he said. He managed to make a fine living out of them, by means of the arts I've mentioned; he took in more in a month than a hundred other blind men do in a year.

And with all that let me tell Your Excellency that I never set eyes on a man who was so close-fisted and stingy. To such a degree that he starved me almost to death and never so much as kept me in the bare necessities. It's the truth: if I hadn't managed to get along on my own wits and ingenuity there were many times when I would have perished of hunger. But with all his experience and shrewdness I found ways to get around him, so that always, or at least most of the time, I collared the lion's share. I played fiendish tricks on him in order to do it—I'll tell you a few of them—though there were times when he caught me and took it out on me.

He carried the bread and everything else besides in a canvas bag which was shut at the top with an iron ring locked with a padlock, and whenever he put anything in or took anything out he did it so carefully and counted everything so precisely that nobody in the world could have stolen a single crumb. And I would take the miserable scrap which he handed me; it never added up to two decent-sized mouthfuls.

Once he had locked the padlock again, when he thought that I was busy at something else he would relax his guard. It was then that I was able, often, to bleed the side of the miserly sack through a place in the seam which I would unpick and then sew up again. I got bread out of it—not a nibble at a time, but good big chunks of it—and pieces of bacon, and sausages. And that way I managed, if not to even up the score, at least to appease the fiendish hunger which that villain of a blind man subjected me to.

Everything which I could pinch or steal I changed into half-pennies. When they got him to make one of his prayers, and gave him pennies, I would take advantage of his not being able to see, and as soon as the penny was held out I would snatch it and pop it into my mouth, and then I would give my master a half-penny instead, which I had ready for the purpose, so that no matter how quickly he grabbed for the penny, thanks to my exchange he never got more than half. The blind villain could tell by the feel that he was not getting whole pennies, and he complained.

"What the devil is going on here?" he said. "Ever since you've been with me they've been giving me nothing but half-pennies. They never used to give me anything smaller than a whole penny, and often it was bigger coins than that. I swear it's your fault that I'm out of luck."

And he would cut his prayers short—in fact he would stop a prayer, unfinished, the moment the person who had ordered it went away. He told me to give his cloak a tug when they left, so he'd know. And I would do it, and then he would start calling again, "Any prayers, anybody? Prayers, anybody?" That was his cry.

He used to put a little jug of wine down beside him when we ate, and I would pick it up without wasting any time about it, and give it a couple of silent kisses and then put it back in its place. But that didn't go on for long. He noticed that there was less wine than there should have been, and after that he never let go of the jug but hung onto it by the handle. But there never was a lodestone which could draw things to itself the way I could. I got a long rye straw and slid it into the mouth of the jug, and with that I sucked up the wine till it had all gone bye-byes. But the old crook was pretty sharp and he must have heard me, because after a while he changed things around and stuck the jug between his legs and put his hand over the top of it. That way he kept his wine safe for himself.

But I was one for the wine, and I got so that I was dying for it. And when I saw that the straw wouldn't work any more, I decided that the best thing would be to make a little hole in the bottom of the jug and cover it up very neatly with a thin wafer of wax. Then when it was time to eat I pretended I was cold and slid between the wretched blind man's legs to warm myself at the miserable little fire we had—which gave out enough heat, just the same, to soften the wax, and since it was very thin, before long the hole started dripping, and by that time I had got my mouth under it, so that not one damned drop got lost. When the old bum went to drink there was nothing there. That surprised him. He couldn't figure it out at all, and he cursed himself and sent jug and wine both to the devil.

"You can't say that it was me drinking it this time, Uncle," I said, "when you've never had your hand off it."

He kept turning the jug over and over, feeling his way around it, until finally he found the hole and caught onto the trick, but didn't let on that he had.

And, so the next day I got the jug-drip going as usual, and settled myself under it without the faintest notion of the troubles that were in store for me and without even suspecting that the blind man had caught onto my trick. I was swallowing gulp after sweet gulp, with my face turned heavenwards and my eyes half shut to get the full taste of that delicious liquor. And that blind monster chose this as the moment to take vengeance upon me. He raised his hands, and with all his strength he brought the jug down on my mouth. I repeat, he did it just as hard as he could. Poor Lazaro! I hadn't been expecting anything of the kind; I was

172

carefree and happy as on former occasions, and it seemed as though the heavens and everything in them had come down on top of me.

That little tap sent things spinning and I was knocked unconscious. He had given me such a tremendous blow with the jug that pieces of it were jammed right into my face, which was gashed all over, and my teeth were broken for good. From that moment on I had it in for that blind man. It was all very well his being nice to me and making a fuss over me and fixing me up where I'd been hurt, I could see that he'd enjoyed inflicting his cruel punishment on me. He put wine on the places where he'd cut my face with the broken jug, and he smiled and said, "What do you think of that, Lazaro? The same thing that got you hurt heals you afterwards and gets you back into shape." And other cracks which weren't to my taste.

When I was halfway to getting over that nasty bash and my bruises I got to thinking that a few more strokes like that one and the blind man would have finished me off once and for all. So I decided to finish him off instead. But I didn't set about it right away. I waited till I could do it safely and make a good job of it. And even though I tried to soothe my anger and forgive him for bashing me with the jug that time, I couldn't because that villainous blind man wouldn't give me a chance. From that day on he treated me abominably. He would hit me for no reason at all, and punch me in the head, and pull my hair.

And if anybody asked him why he abused me that way he'd tell them the story of the jug. He'd say, "You think he's so innocent, just because he's only a boy? Well listen to this and see if you think the devil himself could get up a trick to match it." And they'd cross themselves and say, "Who'd ever have thought it? So little and so wicked!" And they laughed a lot at the trick, and say to him, "Lay into him! Lay into him and God will see you're rewarded." Whereupon he never did anything else.

And for that I always took him over the worst roads, on purpose, just to give him a bad time and make him suffer. If there were any stones around we went that way. If there was any mud I led him through the deepest part. My own feet got a bit damp in the process sometimes, but it was a delight to lose one eye in order to deprive him of both, even though he didn't have any to begin with. As we went he kept shoving the top of his stick against the back of my neck, which was one mass of bruises, and raw with his grabbing me there. I swore I wasn't doing all this deliberately, and that I simply couldn't find roads that were any better, but it didn't help. He wouldn't believe me. He was too wise and sharp for that, the scoundrel.

To give Your Excellency an idea of how crafty this astute blind man was, I will tell you of one incident, among many which occurred while I was with him, which I think gives a good idea of his remarkable cunning. When we left Salamanca he intended to go to the Toledo region, because the people there, as he said, were richer even though they were not particularly openhanded. He backed up his decision with the proverb: "Niggard gives more than naked." And we took the road that led through the most prosperous towns, stopping wherever we got a good reception and had a decent take. At the end of three days if we'd had neither we did a St. John and shook the dust of the place from our feet.

We happened to arrive in a place called Almorox just at the time of the grape harvest, and a grape-picker gave my master a bunch of grapes by way of alms. The grape baskets, as usual, had been banged around a lot and the grapes were very ripe, and as a result the whole thing was falling apart. If he had put it in the sack it would have been ruined and made a mess of everything else. So he decided we should have a feast, partly to get out of having to carry it with us and partly in order to put me in a good humor, because he had been hitting me and kneeing me more than normally that day. We sat down on a wall and he said:

"Now I'm going to be generous to you. We're going to eat this bunch of grapes, and we'll divide it evenly. We'll do it this way: you pick one and then I'll pick one. Only you have to promise me not to take more than one at a time. The same goes for me, and we'll go on that way until they're all gone. That way there won't be any cheating."

So we agreed to that and started in. But the second time around the old cheat broke the rule he'd made and began taking them in twos, thinking, I suppose, that I was doing the same thing. When I saw that he was not sticking to the bargain I wasn't content with just keeping up with him, I had to go him one better. I took to eating them two by two, three by three, or as many as I could get hold of. When we had finished the bunch he sat there with the stem in his hand for a while, and then he shook his head and said:

"Lazarus, you cheated. I would swear to God that you ate those grapes three at a time."

"No I didn't," I said. "What makes you think I did?"

And that wily blind man said, "I know you ate them three at

a time, and I'll tell you how I know. Because I was eating them two at a time and you never said a word."

I didn't have any answer to that.

In Escalona, where we stayed in the house of a shoemaker at about that time, there were a lot of ropes and articles made of hemp hanging down inside a doorway arch which we passed under, and some of them hit my master in the head. He put up his hand and fingered them and felt what they were, and then he said to me:

"Let's go, boy. Let's get away from this: it's a bad dish which chokes without nourishing."

I hadn't noticed anything, and when I looked all I saw was coils of rope and straps of hemp—nothing edible. So I said:

"What do you mean, Uncle?"

He said, "Nephew, not a word. It depends on how you behave yourself whether you come to appreciate the truth of what I said or not."

So we went out from under the portico there and came to an inn where there were a lot of horns on the wall by the door, which were used by the mule-drivers for hitching their pack-animals to. My master came groping along, feeling for the inn where he said a prayer every day for the inn-keeper's wife in her confinement. His hand lighted on one of the horns and he heaved a great sigh and said:

"Oh wicked object, the fruit of worse behavior! How many there are who would like to see you on their neighbors' heads, and yet how few want to have you for themselves, or even want to hear you mentioned in connection with them!"

When I heard that I said, "What do you mean, Uncle?"

"Nephew, not another word. It's a bad dinner and supper I've got in my hand here, but I'll give it to you one of these days."

"I won't eat it," I said, "and you won't give it to me."

"What I've said is true. You'll see, if you live long enough."

So we went on into the doorway of the inn, and I wish to God we'd never got there, because of what happened there.

It was mostly inn-wives, barmaids, candy-sellers, whores, and other little women like that that he prayed for. He hardly ever offered up a prayer for a man. I used to laugh at that. Young as I was, I was struck by the blind man's discretion and prudence.

But I don't want to be long-winded, so I'll skip quite a number of things, amusing and remarkable though they were, which happened to me while I was with my first master, and I'll go on to tell how we came to part, and there I'll leave him. We were in Escalona, the seat of the Duke of Escalona, and there the blind man gave me a piece of sausage to roast. When the sausage had started to drip and he had eaten the drippings he took a coin out of his purse and told me to go to the tavern and fetch him some wine. It's the devil, they say, who makes the thief. And it was the devil who put this next opportunity in my way.

There was a long scrawny miserable turnip lying by the fire where it had been thrown because it wasn't fit for the pot. Since there was nobody there for the moment except him and me, and I had had my appetite whetted by the savory smell of the sausage (which I knew was all that I was going to get of it) I never stopped to think of the possible consequences, but throwing all caution aside in the hope of attaining my desire, I grabbed the sausage while he was fishing the money out of his purse, and put the aforementioned turnip in its place on the spit. Once he'd given me the money my master took hold of the spit and began turning it over the fire, in an effort to roast something which had escaped stewing because of its undesirable qualities.

I went for the wine and made short work of the sausage on the way. When I got back I found the blind old sinner had put the turnip in between two pieces of bread and hadn't realized what it was, because he hadn't touched it with his hand. So when he picked up the bread and bit into it, thinking to get a mouthful of sausage along with it, and got the cold turnip instead, it was a terrible disappointment to him, and he lost his temper and said:

"What's this, Lazaro?"

"Lacerated, you mean," I said. "Why blame me? I've only just brought back the wine, haven't I? Somebody's come and played a trick on you there."

"No, no," he said. "The spit hasn't been out of my hand. So that's impossible."

I lied and swore up and down that I had had nothing to do with that swap but it didn't do me any good because you couldn't keep anything hidden from that cunning blind man. He got up and grabbed me by the head and started smelling me. He must have been using his nose, like a good hound, and got a whiff of my breath and wanted to make sure. He was pretty wrought up, and he snatched my jaw with his hand and pulled my mouth open wider than was good for it and recklessly stuck his nose right in. It was a long nose, and sharp, and at that moment anger had lengthened it by a good hand's breadth. The tip of it touched the back of my throat.

The combination of this and the terrible fear I was in, and both of them right on top of that damned sausage which I'd bolted and which hadn't yet settled in my stomach—but it was mostly the antics of that prodigious nose, which was half choking me—all these put together were responsible for both the deed and the dainty titbit being brought to light, and the owner's property being returned to him. Because before that villainous blind man could get his trunk out of my mouth I became aware of altercations in my stomach, the outcome of which was that my stomach proceeded to give back its stolen goods on the spot, and my master's nose and that damned half-chewed sausage left my mouth together.

Oh God, what I would have given to have been in my grave right then—I was already dead! That perverse blind man flew into such a rage that if the noise hadn't brought some people to my rescue I don't think he'd have left me with my life. They pried me loose from his hands, in which I left my few last hairs. My face was all cut and my neck and throat were scratched. Though my throat deserved it for it was its wickedness that I was suffering for.

That blind old villain told everybody as they arrived about the tricks I'd got up to. He told the same things over and over: the wine-jar, the bunch of grapes, this last one. They all laughed so loud that people going by in the street came in to see what the fun was, and the blind man recounted my doings with so much wit and dash that it seemed wrong of me not to laugh at his stories myself, in spite of my mistreatment and my tears.

And while it was all going on I suddenly thought how weak and cowardly I'd been not to have left him noseless when I had such a good chance that the job, as you might say, was half done. I cursed myself. All I would have had to do was to clamp my teeth shut and he'd have left his nose indoors, and since it belonged to that old scoundrel my stomach might have given it a better reception than it gave the sausage. And when neither of them showed up I could have gone on denying the accusation. I wish to God I'd done it. What a joy it would have been!

The inn-keeper's wife and the other people who'd gathered around made peace between us, and they washed my face and throat with the wine I'd brought for him to drink. The villain plied them with jokes on that subject. He said:

"Honestly, I waste more wine washing this boy in one year than I drink up myself in two. Lazaro, to put it at its very least you owe more to wine than you do to your own father. He only gave you your being once, whereas wine has brought you to life a thousand times."

Then he went on to tell them all the different occasions when he'd whacked me over the head and gouged my face and then fixed me up afterwards with wine.

"I'll tell you," he said, "if there's anyone in this world to whom wine will be a blessing, it will be you."

And the ones who were washing me with the stuff laughed and laughed, however much I cursed and swore. But the blind man's prediction turned out to be the truth itself, and I've often remembered that man since and decided that he must really have had second sight, and I've felt sorry for the mischief I plagued him with. However, I paid him in full for it all, taking into account the truth of what he said that day, as Your Excellency will hear.

What with one thing and another, and the nasty tricks which the blind man had played on me, I had made up my mind to leave him once and for all. And as I had been turning it over in my head and was quite determined to do it, this last caper of his merely strengthened my resolution. The next day, as it happened, we went out into the town to beg for alms. It had rained hard the night before, and it was still raining then, so he went to say his prayers under the arcades which they have there, so that we wouldn't get wet. But as nightfall came on and it was still raining, the blind man said to me:

"This rain acts as though it was never going to stop, Lazaro, and now with the night coming on it's getting worse and worse. Let's get back to the inn while we have a chance."

On the way back we had to cross a gulley which had flooded with the heavy rains. I said to him:

"Uncle, the water's pretty wide here now, but if you like I can see a place where we could cross over more easily without getting wet, because it's much narrower there and we could jump across and not get our feet soaked."

"You're a bright boy, that's why I'm so fond of you. Take me along to where the gulley's narrower. It can be dangerous to get wet in the winter time, especially to get your feet wet."

I could see that my stratagem was working out as I'd hoped it would. I led him out from under the arcade and straight up to a pillar or stone column standing in the square—one of several which support the overhanging eaves of the houses there. Then I said to him:

"Uncle, it's as narrow here as it is anywhere."

It was raining hard and the poor man was getting wet and was in a great hurry for us to get out of the downpour which was soaking us. Add to that what was even more important: God had blinded his intelligence for the time being so that I could work out my vengeance on him. And so he believed me and said:

"Line me up in the right place, and then jump over ahead of me."

I lined him up so that he was facing the pillar. Then I gave a jump and got in back of the column, like somebody waiting for a bull to charge, and I said to him:

"Come on! Jump with all your might and you'll land clear of the water."

I'd hardly finished saying it when the poor blind man hurled himself forward, charging like a billy-goat. He had even taken a step back so as to get a running start and jump better, and he flung himself into the air with all his strength and hit the pillar head-first. It gave out a resounding note as though somebody had hit it with a big calabash, and he fell backward half dead, with his head split open.

"You could smell the sausage," I said to him, "why didn't you smell the post? Smell it now! Smell it now!"

And as there were a lot of people coming to his rescue I left him to their care and maintained a brisk trot till I got to the gates of the town. I was in Torrijos before night. I never found out what God did to him afterwards and I never troubled to make inquiries.

How Lazaro was Employed by a Priest, and What Happened to Him in the Service of that Master

The next day, since I didn't feel safe there, I went on to a place called Maqueda, where for my sins I fell in with a priest. I went and asked him for alms and he asked me if I knew how to assist at mass. I said I did, which was the truth. Because for all he abused me, the blind sinner had taught me a great many things, and that among them. In the end the priest employed me.

I'd got away from the thunder only to be struck by lightning. The blind man, as big a miser and all as he was, as I've said, was Alexander the Great compared to this one. All I can say is that my new master had collected all the stinginess in the world and was hoarding it. Whether he had been born with that character or had put it on with his priest's cassock I don't know.

He had an old chest which he kept locked, and he carried the key on a string tied to his robe. When the holy bread came out of the church he would pop it into the chest, which he then locked up again. And unlike other houses, where there is usually a side of bacon hanging in the chimney or a bit of cheese somewhere on a table or in a cupboard, or a basket with a few pieces of bread in it left over from the last meal, in that house there was nothing to eat anywhere. I'm sure that even if I hadn't eaten any, the mere sight of a few things of that kind would have been comforting.

All that was there was one string of onions and that was under lock and key in a room at the top of the house. I was supposed to have one of those onions every four days as my ration, and when I asked him for the key, to go and get it, if there was anyone else present he would slip his hand into his inside pocket and with an air of long-suffering produce the key and hand it to me, saying:

"There you are. Bring it back when you're finished. You never do anything but stuff yourself with sweetmeats."

As though all the jams and jellies in Valencia had been locked up there, when, as I've said, there wasn't a damned thing in the whole room but those onions hanging from a nail. And he kept such a close count of those that if, sinner that I am, I had taken more than my allotted share, I would have paid for it dearly.

In the end I was dying of hunger. But though he wasn't very charitable with me, he was a bit more so when it came to himself. He spent five pence a day, as a regular thing, on meat for his dinner and supper. It's true, he shared the broth with me. But as for the meat itself, not a whisker. All I got was a little piece of bread, and I wish to God it had been even half enough.

On Sundays in that part of the country they have sheep's head. He sent me for one—it cost a bit more than his weekday allowance. He cooked it and ate the eyes, the tongue, the neck, the brains, and the cheek, and he gave me the gnawed bones, saying:

"Go on, take it! Eat up! Celebrate! The world is yours! You live better than the Pope!"

"God reward you the same way," I said to myself.

After three weeks with him I was so feeble with hunger that I couldn't stand up straight. It was as plain as could be that I was on my way to the grave if God and my own wits didn't find some way to help me out. There was no chance to put my gifts to any use, for there wasn't anything to steal. Even if there had been, I couldn't have hoodwinked him as I did my first master, whom may God forgive if that bash on the head finished him off. For clever though he was, he'd lacked that one sense, and as a result he wasn't able to keep tabs on me, whereas this other had the sharpest eyes ever made.

At the offertory there wasn't a penny dropped into the bowl but he registered it. He kept one eye on the worshippers and one on my hands, and his eyes danced in their sockets like quicksilver. He had every penny counted. And once the offering had all been collected he took the bowl from me and put it on the altar.

I wasn't man enough to pinch one penny from him the whole time I was living with him—or dying with him would be a better way of putting it. I never fetched him one penny's worth of wine from the tavern, because what little he got from the offering was put into the chest and he spun it out by degrees so that it lasted him all week.

And in order to cover up his terrible stinginess he said to me:

"You see, boy, priests are supposed to be extremely temperate in their eating and drinking. That's why I don't go indulging in excesses, like other people."

But he was lying, the miserable creature, because when we went to pray at meetings and wakes, where somebody else was paying, he ate like a wolf and drank more than a quack doctor.

And speaking of wakes, God forgive me, I was never a foe to humanity except on those occasions. Because then we ate well and I stuffed myself. I yearned, I actually prayed to God to kill off one of His servants every day. And when we went to give the sacrament to the sick, especially when it was Extreme Unction, when the priest asks everybody present to pray I wasn't the last to start. I prayed to the Lord with all my heart and with a right good will, but I didn't ask Him to dispose of the person according to His will, as they usually do. I begged that the object of our prayers might be removed from this world.

And when one of them got better, God forgive me, I wished him to the devil a thousand times over. But if he died I pronounced a like number of blessings on his soul. Because in all the time that I was with the priest, which was nearly six months, only twenty people died, and I'm convinced that I killed them, or put it this way, that they died at my request. Because I believe that the Lord beheld my famished and continual descent toward the grave, and that it pleased Him to kill them off in order to keep me alive. But there was no remedy for my sufferings at that time. Because even though I made out alright on funeral days, on the others when nobody had died and I had gone back to my everyday hunger, I found it even harder to bear because I had known what it was to be full and had got used to it. So really there was no ease for me except death, and sometimes I desired it not only for others but for myself too. But though I felt it inside me the whole time it never carried me off.

I often considered leaving that skinflint of a master, but there were two things which kept me there. First, I couldn't count on my legs, they had got so weak from sheer hunger. And second, thinking things over I said to myself:

"I've had two masters. The first one nearly starved me to death and when I left him I took up with this one who's virtually brought me to the edge of the grave. If I quit this one now and land myself with another one who's even worse, there's only one thing that can happen to me: I'll die."

So I didn't dare to clear out, because I was absolutely convinced that any step would be a step down. And if I went any lower than I was, that would be the last anybody would ever hear of Lazaro in this world.

May the Lord preserve all faithful Christians from such affliction as I suffered then, for I didn't know what to think or what to do, and obviously I was going from bad to worse. Well, one day when that miserable, low, contemptible wretch my master was out of town, a tinker happened to come to the door. It's my opinion that he was really an angel disguised as a tinker, who had been sent to me there by the hand of God himself. He asked me whether there was anything that needed fixing.

"There's plenty of repair work to be done just on me, and you'd be doing well if you could patch me up," I said, but under my breath so he couldn't hear me.

But this wasn't the moment to waste time in witticisms, and the Holy Ghosts inspired me just then and I said:

"Uncle, I've lost the key to this chest and I'm afraid my master will beat me. Please, I beseech you, see if one of the ones you've got with you will fit, and I'll pay you for it."

The angelic tinker took the big bunch of keys which he was carrying and started trying them one after the other, and I helped him with my feeble prayers. Before I realized it I saw the face of God in the form of bread, as they say—loaf after loaf of it, inside the chest. When it was open I said:

"I haven't any money to pay you for the key, but there, pay yourself out of what's in the chest."

He took one of the loaves of bread, the one which looked best to him, and gave me the key, and went away very happy, leaving me even more so.

But for the moment I didn't touch anything, because I didn't want the loss to be discovered. Besides, the mere knowledge that I was the lord and master of such treasures seemed to keep my hunger at bay. My stingy master came back and it pleased God not to let him miss the loaf which the angel had taken.

The next day when he left the house I opened my bready paradise and got my hands and teeth onto a loaf and in the time it takes to say the creed twice I'd made it invisible, and I didn't forget to lock up the chest afterwards. Then I started to sweep the house, happy as could be, thinking that I'd found the way to make things a bit better for myself in the future. I went on rejoicing in this thought all that day and the next. But I wasn't fated to enjoy that relief for long. On the third day I had a relapse, and a severe one.

When I least expected it, suddenly I stumbled on him who was starving me to death, bent over the coffer, rummaging the contents, tumbling them around, and counting the loaves of bread over and over. I pretended not to notice, but I prayed three kinds of prayers, in all of them repeating, "Saint John, strike him blind!"

When he'd been a long time counting them by days and by fingers, he said:

"If this chest weren't so securely locked I'd say that there were several loaves of bread missing. But from today on I'll shut out this suspicion and keep a more careful count. There are nine left and a piece of another."

"God send you nine troubles," I said to myself.

I felt as though his words had gone through me like a hunter's arrow, and my stomach was harrowed with hunger at the very thought of returning to my former diet. He went out of the house, and to console myself I opened the chest, and when I caught sight of the bread I fell to worshipping it, without daring to receive it (as they say at Holy Communion). I counted the loaves to see whether the miserable wretch could have made a mistake, by any chance, and I found his count more accurate than I would have liked. The best I could do was to cover them with kisses and to remove as delicately as I could a little bit of the crust from the broken-off side. I had to make do with that for that day, and I wasn't as happy as I had been the day before.

But I got more and more famished, and my hunger was aggravated by the fact that on the two or three days which I've spoken of I had got into the habit of having a bit more bread to eat. I was dying a terrible death. It got so bad that the only thing I ever did when I was left to myself was to open and shut the chest and contemplate the face of God inside it, as the children say. But God, who helps those who are in trouble, saw the dreadful state I was in and led me to stumble on a way of somewhat improving my situation. For as I was turning it over in my mind, I said:

"This chest is big, and old, and there are holes in it here and there even though they aren't very big. There's no reason why he shouldn't believe that mice had got in and been at the bread. It wouldn't be a good idea to take out a whole loaf because he'd miss it—trying to keep me on nothing at all! Well, I'll survive."

And I started to crumble the bread onto a couple of not very sumptuous tablecloths there. I took up one loaf and put down another, and so on until I'd crumbled a little from each of them; there were three or four. Then I ate the crumbs, savoring them as though they were candy, and they made me feel a little better. But when he came to eat and opened the chest he saw the mess that had been made in there and obviously he thought it was mice that had done the damage, because I had made it look exactly the way mice leave things. He looked all over the chest from one end to the other and he found the holes and figured that they must have got in there. He called me, and said:

"Look, Lazaro! Look at the calamity which befell our bread last night!"

I pretended to be amazed and asked him what could have happened.

"Mice," he said. "What else? Nothing on earth is safe from them."

We sat down to eat and it was God's will that even here I should be in luck, for I got more bread than the miserable creature usually gave me. He took his knife and cut off the part which he thought the mice had been at, saying:

"There, eat that. The mouse is a clean animal."

And thus, with my ration supplemented by the labor of my hands, or rather of my nails, we finished that day's eating before I'd really got started.

And afterwards I had another shock. I saw him rummaging around industriously pulling nails out of the walls and hunting up pieces of board which he nailed over the holes in the old chest to block them up.

Then I said, "Oh my God! What misery and misfortune and disasters we mortals have to undergo, and how brief are the pleasures of this our toilsome life! Here I thought, with this wretched and pitiful dodge, that I was going to be able to improve the utter indigence of my situation and make things bearable, and I was already happy, rejoicing in my good fortune. But my luck wouldn't stand it, and roused my wretch of a master and put him even more on his guard than he is normally—and misers are seldom noted for their carelessness. Now in blocking up the holes in the chest he's shutting the door on my consolation and opening it to all my troubles."

And I went on lamenting in this way, while my busy carpenter brought his labors to an end, using nail after nail and board after board, and saying:

"Now sirs, you sneaking mice will have to work out something else, for you'll have no luck in this house."

As soon as he was gone I went to inspect his handiwork, and I found that he hadn't left a hole big enough to let a mosquito in, anywhere in that wretched old chest. I opened it with my now useless key, without any hope of getting anything out of it, and I looked at the loaves which my master thought the mice had been nibbling. I managed to get a little bit more off them just the same, touching them very lightly, like a skilful fencer. After all, necessity is the best teacher, and I was never at a loss for that; night and day I never stopped thinking of ways to keep alive. And I'm convinced that hunger was the light which led me to these miserable expedients, for they say that hunger rouses the wits and satiety does the opposite, and certainly that was the case with me.

One night when I was lying awake turning it over and over in my mind, trying to think of a way to take advantage of that chest and make use of it, I could tell that my master was asleep because he was snoring and giving out a series of loud snorts, which he never did except in his sleep. I got up without making a sound. I had decided that day on what to do, and I had taken an old knife which was lying around and had put it where I could find it. I went over to the wretched chest, and in a place where I had noticed that its defenses seemed weakest, I applied the knife to it and started boring into the wood. The chest was a very old one indeed, and its countless years, as I found, had left it without either the strength or the heart to resist. Instead, it was soft and rotten, and it gave way in no time and allowed me to make a good sized hole in its side, for my own good. Once this was done I opened the wounded chest very quietly and groped around until I got the broken piece of bread, and I gave it the same treatment which I have described above. This made me feel a little better, and I shut the chest behind me and went back to my straw, where I got some rest and a little sleep.

But I didn't sleep well, which I attributed to not having had enough to eat. It must have been that, because at that time all the worries of the King of France couldn't have kept me awake.

The next day my lord and master noticed the damage. He found the hole and saw that there was some bread missing, and he started cursing the mice, and said:

"What's to be said about this? There were never any mice in this house until now!"

Which no doubt was the truth. For if they had decided to spare one house out of the whole kingdom they would have picked that one, and rightly, for they don't usually stay where there isn't anything to eat. He started going through the house again, hunting up boards and pulling nails out of the walls to block up the holes. As soon as night came, and its rest, I was ready with my old knife, and as often as he blocked them up in the daytime I unblocked them at night.

So it went on, and we kept it up at a great rate, fulfilling the old saying that "Where one door shuts another opens." In fact it was as though we were hard at work on Penelope's loom—what he wove in the daytime I undid at night. After a few days and nights the poor larder looked such a wreck that it would have been hard to say what it was. You'd scarcely have called it a chest. It looked more like an old breastplate from another age, what with the nails and tacks stuck into it everywhere.

When he realized that all his efforts were to no avail, he said:

"This chest is so battered, and the wood is so old and flimsy that any mouse could force his way in. And the way it's going, if it gets any worse it won't afford any protection at all. Worse still, though it's not much use, if I were to get rid of it I'd find it hard to do without and it would cost me three or four *reales* to replace it. The best thing I can think of, since nothing else has worked so far, is to rig up a trap inside it for the accursed little beasts."

Then he went and asked around and borrowed a mouse trap and begged a few cheese parings from the neighbors, and with these he fixed up a man-made cat which he kept set in the chest. Which was a big help to me. For though I didn't need any sauces to whip up my appetite, nevertheless I enjoyed the cheese parings which I removed from the trap, but I didn't let them distract me from my mousy treatment of the bread.

When he found that the bread had been nibbled and the cheese eaten too, and that the offending mouse had still not been caught, he cursed and swore and asked the neighbors what it could be that ate the cheese, taking it out of the trap without getting caught or imprisoned even though the door of the trap had fallen shut.

The neighbors all agreed that it couldn't have been a mouse that had done the damage because a mouse would have been caught at some point or another. One of them said:

"I remember that there used to be a snake near your house. That's probably what it is. It stands to reason: it's long, so it would be able to take the bait, and even though the door of the trap were to fall shut on it, since its whole body wouldn't be inside, it would be able to get out again."

They all agreed with what he said, and my master was very upset. After that he slept much less soundly, and any noise he heard at night which sounded like wood being bored he thought was the snake gnawing at the chest, and he was on his feet in a second, with a big club which he'd kept at the head of his bed ever since they'd told him that. And with this weapon he'd belabor the poor old chest, to scare away the snake. He woke the neighbors with the racket he made, and he didn't let me get much sleep. He would come over to the straw where I was lying and fling it this way and that way, and me with it, on the chance that the snake might have come in my direction and got into my straw or my jacket. Because they'd told him that at night these creatures have a way of crawling into children's cradles, in search of warmth, occasionally biting them and proving dangerous.

Usually I pretended to be asleep, and in the morning he would say to me:

"Didn't you hear anything last night, boy? I went after the snake. It wouldn't surprise me if it had got into your bed, because they're cold-blooded creatures, and they look for warmth."

"I hope to God he doesn't bite me," I said. "The very thought of him scares me to death."

He was so strung up and jumpy with all this that he never seemed to doze off, and consequently the so-called snake never dared to approach the chest at night to do any nibbling. But I took to raiding in the daytime, while he was in the church or out in the town. When he discovered the damage and realized that his efforts had had no effect at all, he spent the nights prowling around like a ghost.

I was afraid that with all this watchfulness he would stumble on the key which I'd hidden under the straw, and I thought it would be safer to put it in my mouth. As a matter of fact ever since I had lived with the blind man I had been using it as a change-purse, until by now I could keep twelve or fifteen *maravedis* in it, all in half-penny pieces, without their getting in the way of my eating. Otherwise I would never have had a penny to call my own, but that damned old blind man would have come across it, for he used to search every seam and patch in my clothing down to the last stitch.

So as I say, every night I put the key into my mouth and went to sleep without worrying about my warlock of a master finding it; but when misfortune is on its way precautions are useless. My fates, or I should say my sins, were pleased to ordain that one night as I was asleep, having put the key in my mouth, my mouth must have dropped open in such a way, and into such a position, that the wind of my breath as I exhaled in my sleep passed through the hollow-tubed shaped part of the key, and as my approaching disaster would have it, the key gave out a loud hissing sound. My master heard it and it gave him a fright. Apparently he thought it was the snake hissing. No doubt that was what it sounded like.

He got up very quietly with his club in his hand and groped his way over toward the sound and came to where I was. He didn't make any noise for fear the snake would hear him. As he got closer it occurred to him that the creature must have crawled into the straw where I was lying in order to take advantage of my warmth. He raised the stick as high as he could, meaning to bring it down on the snake and deal it a death-blow. Then he swung the club with all his might and landed it squarely on me and it knocked me unconscious and split my head open.

He realized at once what he had done, for it seems that I groaned and moaned terribly as a result of that ferocious blow. He said that he bent over me and called to me in a loud voice, trying to bring me back to my senses. But when he touched me with his hands he could feel blood all over me, and then he knew that he must have really injured me. And he hurried and got a light and brought it, and found me moaning, with the key still in my mouth. I had never let go of it. Half of it was still sticking out just as it must have been when it had made the hissing noise.

The snake-killer was surprised to see it, and stared at it, wondering what it could be. Then he took it out of my mouth and saw what it was and found that it was exactly the same shape as his. He went and tried it, and so he got to the bottom of my mystifications.

Probably the cruel hunter said:

"Now I've found the mouse and the snake who gave me no peace and were eating me out of house and home."

I can't swear to anything that happened during the next three days, for I spent them in the belly of the whale, but everything which I've just set down I heard from my master's lips, for he recounted it in some detail to everybody who came along.

After three days I regained consciousness and found myself lying on my straw with my head covered in plasters and larded with oils and unguents, and I was terrified and said:

"What's all this?"

The cruel priest answered:

"The truth is that I've hunted down the mice and the snakes that were practically the ruination of me."

I looked myself over and saw how battered I was, and then the extent of my misfortune dawned on me.

Just then an old woman who did healing came in, and some neighbors. And they started to take the bandages off my head and doctor the place where I'd been clubbed. They were pleased to find that I'd regained consciousness, and they said:

"Now that he's restored to his senses God will see that he gets over it."

And they started recounting my troubles again and laughing over them. But I, poor sinner, cried over them. Anyway they gave me something to eat, for I was so faint with hunger that their other ministrations were hardly any good to me. And as a result, little by little I got stronger until at the end of two weeks I got up and was out of danger—though I was still hungry—and halfway to recovery.

The day after I got up my lord and master took me by the hand and led me out the door and into the street and said to me:

"Lazaro, from today on you serve yourself, not me. Go find yourself a master and God be with you, for I don't want to have such a diligent servant living with me. I'd swear you'd been a blind man's boy."

And making the sign of the cross against me as though I had been possessed of a devil, he went back into the house and shut the door.

How Lazaro was Employed by a Squire, and What Happened to Him with that Master

And so I had no choice but to muster up strength out of weakness, and little by little, with the help of kind people I made my way to this famous city of Toledo, where by the mercy of God, in two weeks my wound had healed up. And as long as there was something the matter with me people gave me alms, but once I was better they all said to me:

"You're a rascal and a good-for-nothing! Go find yourself a good master and work for him."

"Find a good master! Where?" I asked myself. "Unless God were to make one from scratch, as He made the world!"

So I went rambling on from door to door (and precious little good it did me, for charity had gone to heaven) and as I did, God put me in the way of a squire who was walking down the street. He was passably dressed, well groomed, and his bearing and manner were all that they should have been. He looked at me and I looked at him, and he said to me:

"Are you looking for a master, boy?"

I said:

"Yes, sir."

"Well, follow me, then," he said. "God has been good to you, fixing things so that you'd meet me. You must have said a good prayer today."

So I followed him, thanking God for what I heard him say, and also because, judging by his clothes and his demeanor, he seemed to be just the man I was looking for.

It was in the morning that I met my third master. He led me across the greater part of the city. We crossed squares where they were selling bread and other provisions. I expected, in fact I longed for him to load me up with what they had for sale, for it was the hour for marketing, when people usually shop for what's needed, but he hurried past all of those things.

"Maybe he doesn't like the look of things here," I said, "and we're going to do the shopping somewhere else."

So we went on walking till it struck eleven. Then he went into the cathedral, and I right behind him, and he heard mass and the other divine offices, while I watched. His manner was very devout. He stayed till it was all over and everybody had gone. Then we went out of the church.

At the same smart clip as before we started down one of the streets. I was the happiest person in the world to see that we weren't bothering to do any shopping for food. I had decided that my new master was obviously a man who bought things in quantities, and that his meal was probably all ready and was exactly what I needed and was pining for.

As we went along the clock struck one in the afternoon, and we came to a house in front of which my master stopped, and I with him. Hitching his cloak to the left, he drew a key from his sleeve and opened the door, and we went into the house. It was so dark and dismal in the room just inside the door that it might have been made that way on purpose to frighten people as they came in, but it opened into a little patio and a number of decent-sized rooms.

Once we were inside he took off his cloak and asked me whether my hands were clean; then we shook it out and folded it. And then very fastidiously he blew the dust off a stone bench there and laid the cloak down on it. Having taken care of that, he sat down next to it and asked me endless questions about where I came from and how I had happened to come to that city.

It took me longer to tell the whole story than I would have liked, because to my mind, at that hour it would have been more proper for me to have been setting the table and dishing up the stew, instead of supplying his curiosity. However, I satisfied him on the subject of myself insofar as my talent for lying permitted. I expatiated upon my good points and kept quiet about everything else, for I didn't feel it was the moment for intimacies. When I had finished he sat there without moving for a while, and I took that for a bad sign. There it was, nearly two o'clock and he gave no evidence of having any more appetite than a corpse.

Then I began to ponder over his locking the door behind us, and over the fact that I hadn't yet heard the footsteps of a living person either above or below us anywhere in the house. I'd seen nothing but walls, and not a single chair among them, nor stool, nor bench, nor table, nor even a chest like my old stand-by. I ended up thinking the place must be under an enchantment. And just as I came to this conclusion, he said to me:

"Have you eaten, boy?"

"No sir," I said, "for it hadn't struck eight yet when I met you."

"Well, even at that hour I had already had my breakfast, and let me tell you, if I have partaken of anything at all in the morning that way, I never touch another thing until nightfall. So get along as best you can, and we'll have supper later on."

Your Excellency may well believe that when I heard this I nearly fell down in a faint, and it wasn't just from hunger, it was the certain knowledge that fortune was dead set against me. Everything that I had endured came back to me, and at the thought of my hardships I began to cry. I remembered the considerations that had held me when I had thought of leaving the priest, and how I'd told myself that however miserable and miserly he was, I might take up with somebody worse. In short, I cried for the hardships of my past life, and my death which could not be far in the future.

But with all that I dissimulated as well as I could, and said:

"Sir, I'm only a boy and I don't mind much about eating, thank God. I can boast that I have a smaller appetite than any of my colleagues—all the masters that I have had up until now have praised me on that account."

"That certainly is a virtue," he said, "and I will be more warmly attached to you because of it. Stuffing is a pursuit for pigs, and men who have any self-respect should eat moderately."

"Oh, I know what you mean alright!" I said to myself. "And to hell with all the medicinal qualities and other virtues which every master I take up with manages to find in hunger."

I settled myself right by the door and from inside my shirt I extracted a few pieces of bread which were left out of the alms which I'd been given in the name of God. When he saw this he said:

"Come here, boy. What are you eating?"

I went over to him and showed him the bread. There were three pieces. He took the biggest and best and said to me:

"I swear, this looks like good bread."

"Indeed," I said, "do you think so now, sir?"

"I certainly do," he said. "Where did you get it? I wonder whether it was kneaded by clean hands."

"I wouldn't know anything about that," I said to him, "but it tastes perfectly edible to me."

"God grant you're right," said my poor master.

And lifting it to his mouth he started wolfing it in huge mouthfuls, while I attacked another piece in the same way.

"By God," he said, "it's delicious bread."

But by then I'd worked out which foot he limped on, and I wasn't wasting any time. Because I could see that if he finished before I did he was of a mind to help me get through what was left.

So we finished up neck and neck. Then my master set about flicking off a few crumbs which had fallen onto his shirt—only very tiny crumbs, though. After that he went into a little room there and brought out a jug. It was all chipped and it was not very new. And when he had drunk he invited me to do the same. But I was keeping up the temperance act, and I said:

"I never touch wine, sir."

"It's water," he said. "You can drink that alright."

So I took the jug and drank. Not much, because thirst wasn't my problem.

And that was that until nightfall. We went on talking of things which he asked me about, and I answered his questions as well as I could. As time wore on he took me into the room from which he'd got the jug, and said to me:

"Boy, you go there and watch how we make this bed, so that you'll know how to do it from now on."

I stood at one end and he at the other and we made the wretched bed. There wasn't much of it to make. It consisted of a couple of benches with a wickerwork frame on top of them. And then the bed-clothes, laid over a miserable mattress. Which mattress had been spared from washing for so long that it wasn't recognizable as a mattress at all, but he'd gone on using it, even though there was somewhat less wool in it than there was meant to be. We smoothed it out and did our best to make it softer. Which wasn't possible because what's naturally hard can't be softened. And that damned pack-saddle did not have one blessed thing inside it. When we laid it on top of the wickerwork you could make out every single reed underneath, so that what it looked most like was the backbone of a starving hog. And on that famished mattress there was a quilt out of the same litter, whose color I could never quite make out.

When the bed had been made and night was upon us, he said to me:

"Lazaro, it's late, and it's quite a way from here to the market. Besides, the city is full of thieves who do their cloak-and-dagger work at night. Let's get along as best we can, and tomorrow, once the daylight is here, God will be good to us. I'm all by myself so I hadn't got anything laid in; I've been eating out for the last three days. But now we'll have to make other arrangements."

"Oh, as for me, sir," I said, "set your mind at rest. I'm capable of going without food for a night, or even longer if necessary."

"You'll live longer and keep your health better," he answered. "Because as we were saying, there's nothing in all the world like eating little to make you live long."

"If that's the way of it," I said to myself, "I'll live forever, because I've kept that rule religiously, and for that matter I expect I'll have the bad luck to keep it for the rest of my life."

He lay down on the bed, using his breeches and his doublet as a pillow, and he told me to lie down at his feet, which I did. But not a blessed wink of sleep did I get! The reeds and my protruding bones took to bickering and brawling and never left off the whole night. For what with my hardships and sufferings and lack of nourishment I don't think there was a pound of flesh on my body, and besides, having eaten nothing all day, I was enduring all the torments of hunger, which is no friend of sleep. God forgive me, I cursed myself and my miserable fortune a thousand times, through the greater part of that night. Worse than that, I didn't dare turn over for fear of waking him up, and many is the time I prayed to God for death.

When the morning came we got up and he started in dusting off and shaking out his breeches, doublet, jacket and cloak. And I played the part of his valet! He wasn't in any hurry to get dressed; he took his time. I poured water for him to wash his hands, and he combed his hair and strapped on his sword belt and as he did it he said to me:

"Oh, if you knew what a treasure this is, my lad! The gold piece that could buy it from me doesn't exist. There isn't one among all the blades turned out by the most famous swordsmith in Toledo which has edges on it as sharp as these."

And he drew it from its sheath and tried it with two fingers, saying:

"You see? I'd lay a bet that I could cut through a skein of wool with this."

I said to myself:

"Yes, and with nothing but my teeth, and they aren't even steel, I could go through a four pound loaf."

He sheathed it and buckled it on and draped a string of fat beads through his sword belt. And with an easy-going amble, holding himself very straight and moving both his body and his head smoothly and gracefully, flicking the end of his cloak over his shoulder one minute and under his arm the next, but with his right hand permanently on his side, he went out the door, saying:

"Lazaro, see to the house while I'm at Mass, and make the bed and fill the water jug at the river which is right down there, and lock the door so that nothing gets stolen from us, and put the key here by the hinge so that I can get in when I come back."

And up the street he went, with such a well-bred, graceful air and bearing that anybody who saw him must surely have taken him for a near relative of the Count of Alarcos, or at the very least his chamberlain.

"The Lord be blessed," I said to myself when I was left alone, for He sends the cure as well as the disease. To see this gentleman, now, and his airs and graces, anyone would think that he'd had a fine supper last night, and slept in a good bed, and they'd suppose that he'd eaten a hearty breakfast, too, early as it is. Who wouldn't be fooled by his presentable appearance and perfectly respectable cloak and jacket? And who would dream that that same respectably turned-out gentleman had spent the whole of yesterday without a bite to eat except for the crust of bread which his servant Lazaro had carried around for a day and a night sequestered in the front of his shirt where it hadn't got any cleaner? And that today he had washed his hands and face and then, for want of a towel, had had to use his shirttail? Nobody would so much as suspect it, I'm sure. Oh Lord, how many of this sort must there be scattered through the world, suffering things for the moldy misery they call honor which they would never suffer for Thee!"

I stood in the doorway musing and thinking over these things and many others until my master had disappeared down the long narrow street. And once he was out of sight I went back into the house and before you could have said the creed I'd been over the whole place, from top to bottom: there was nothing to stop me— and nothing to stop for. I made the miserable hard bed and took the jug and myself to the river, where I caught sight of my master, in a garden, having an animated conversation with two women in veils, who looked to be the sort who are never in short supply in that section of town. Quite a few of them have adopted the fashion of sallying out there onto the cool river banks on summer mornings to refresh themselves and have lunch without the bother of taking any with them. They simply trust that somebody will come along and provide for them: the gentlemen of the town have got them to taking it for granted.

And as I say, there he was in their company, become a regular gallant, as courtly as Macias ever was, and plying them with more sweet nothings than Ovid ever wrote. When he had got them to understand how tenderly inclined he was, they weren't too shy to ask him for lunch, at the usual price.

But his purse was as cold as his stomach was hot, and at their words he was seized with such a chill that all the color went out of his face and he started to trip over his tongue and to make excuses which anybody could have seen through.

They'd been around, obviously. They could see what was the matter with him, and they left him for what he was.

I was chewing on some cabbage stalks at the time, by way of breakfast. I conducted myself very dutifully, as a new servant should, and went back to the house before my master set eyes on me. I thought I'd sweep the place a little, because it certainly needed it, but I couldn't find anything to do it with. I tried to think what to do, and it seemed to me that the best thing would be to wait until noon for my master, in case he should come back bringing something for us to eat. But that was a vain hope.

When I saw that it was two o'clock and he still hadn't come back, and I was going through tortures of hunger, I shut the door and put the key where he'd told me to, and went back to plying my old trade. In a low sickly voice, with my hands drooping over my breast with God in front of my eyes and His name on my tongue, I set about begging bread at the doorways of whichever big houses looked most promising. It was a calling which I'd sucked in with my mother's milk; what I mean is, I'd learned it in my youth from a great master, the blind man, and I'd turned out to be such a good pupil that though there was scant charity in that town and it had not been a very prosperous year, I was able to work the art to very good effect, so that before the clock struck four I had as many pounds of bread stowed away inside me and another two tucked into my sleeves and the front of my shirt. I went back to the lodging and on the way I passed a tripe stall and I went and begged from one of the women there and she gave me a piece of cow's foot and a few scraps of cooked tripe.

When I got to the house my good master was there ahead of me, with his cloak folded and laid on the stone bench; he was walking back and forth in the patio. As I entered he came over to me. I thought he was going to scold me for being late, but God had better things in store.

He asked me where I'd been.

I said to him: "Sir, I waited here for you until two o'clock, and when Your Excellency hadn't come back by then I went out into the city to commend myself to the good people, and, as you see, they gave me this."

I showed him the bread and the tripe, which was wrapped in my shirttail. His face brightened when he saw these, and he said:

"Well, I waited dinner for you, but then when you didn't come, I ate. However, you've borne yourself like a respectable person in this, for it's better to beg in God's name than it is to steal. May God deny me His grace if I don't think what you did was a fine thing. Only I must implore you not to let on that you live with me. Because of my honor. Though I don't suppose anyone knows that you live here, for I'm barely known in this city. I wish to God I'd never set foot in it!"

"Put your mind at rest, sir, as far as that's concerned," I said to him, "for there's not a damned soul needs to ask me about it, and I won't tell them."

"Now then, eat, poor sinner. For, God willing, we'll soon be free of want. Though I may tell you that nothing has gone right for me since I first came into this house. It must be built on unlucky ground. For there are houses which are ill-omened and unlucky, and they bring bad luck on the people who live in them. I'm pretty sure that this is one of those. But I swear to you that once the month is up I wouldn't stay in it if they gave it to me."

I sat down on the end of the stone bench and I didn't mention the lunch which I'd had, for fear he should take me for a glutton. And I started in to dine and chew on my tripe and bread, meanwhile watching my wretched master without appearing to do so. He never took his eyes off my shirttail, which at that moment I was using as a plate. God pity me as deeply as I pitied him, because I had felt just what he was feeling, and had been through it many many times, day after day. I wondered whether it would be quite proper for me to ask him to join me, but since he'd told me that he'd already eaten, I was afraid he wouldn't accept my invitation. I simply wanted the wretched man to add his efforts to my own and break his fast with me as he had done the day before. And the situation was more favorable to it this time, because the food was better and I wasn't so hungry.

It pleased God to grant my wish. I think it was my master's

wish too. Because I had scarcely started to eat when he stopped his striding back and forth and came over to me and said:

"You know, Lazaro, you have such an elegant way of eating, I never in my life saw any man's that could compare with it. Nobody could watch you eat without it giving him an appetite whether he had one before or not."

"The splendor of your own appetite," I said to myself, "lends beauty to mine."

However, I thought I should help him out, for he was trying hard himself and had given me an opening, and I said to him:

"Sir, the better the tools the better the workman. This bread is absolutely delicious, and this cow's foot is so exquisitely cooked and seasoned that a taste of it would tempt anybody."

"Did you say cow's foot?"

"Yes sir."

"I tell you, it's the choicest titbit in the world. I'd rather have it than pheasant."

"Well taste it, sir, and you'll see how good it is."

I gave him the cow's knuckle to hold in his, and three or four hunks of the whitest bread along with it. He sat down beside me and started to eat like somebody who has a real appetite, gnawing every little particle of bone cleaner than I ever saw a greyhound do.

"This is marvellous with a garlic sauce," he said.

"You're eating it with a better sauce than that," I answered, under my breath.

"By God, it tasted as good as though I hadn't had a bite to eat all day."

"Give me good years and many of them as surely as that's true," I said to myself.

He asked for the jug of water and I gave it to him just as I'd fetched it. None of it had been drunk, and I took that as a fair sign that my master hadn't had too much to eat. We drank and, feeling much better, we went to bed as we'd done the night before.

To make a long story short, we went on in this way for a week or ten days: the wretched man went out every morning with that same pampered expression, at that same stately pace, to swallow air in the streets while Lazaro did his hunting for him.

I kept thinking about what bad luck I'd had: how in escaping from the dreadful masters whom I'd served, and looking for a better one, I'd stumbled upon one who not only neglected to provide for me but could not have done it if he had wanted to.

And for all that I was quite fond of him because I could see that he didn't own a thing and couldn't have done any better. I was more inclined to pity him than to resent him. And on many occasions I did without, myself, so that I'd have something to take back to the lodging for him to get along on.

Because one morning when the poor wretch got out of bed with nothing on but his shirt and went upstairs to relieve himself I decided to find out once and for all, and I unfolded his doublet and breeches, which he had left at the head of the bed, and I found a velvet purse in them, all crumpled and creased and without a single blessed penny inside it, nor any sign that there'd been one there for some time.

"He's poor," I said to myself, "and nobody can give what he hasn't got. Whereas that miserly blind man and that niggardly skin-flint of a priest had both done alright for themselves in the name of God, the one with his hand-kissing and the other with his line of patter, and they starved me half to death. So it's perfectly fair to be down on them and to take pity on this one."

God is my witness that to this day whenever I run across somebody who conducts himself like that and strides and struts around that way, I'm sorry for him and wonder whether he's as hard up as my master was. Whom I would rather have worked for than for my previous masters in spite of his poverty, for the reasons I have given. I had only one little complaint, as far as he was concerned. I would have been happier if he hadn't been quite so pretentious, if he had reduced his vanity just a little as his needs increased. But as nearly as I can figure out that's the rule among people of that sort, and they keep to it. Even if they haven't got a brass farthing they have to have their hats on just so. May the Lord help them, because if He doesn't their affliction is likely to prove fatal.

Well, such was the state of my affairs, and I was leading the life I have described, when my evil star, which was never tired of persecuting me, decided to put an end to that difficult and dishonorable arrangement. As it turned out, that year the crops had failed in that part of the country, and the city government decreed that all paupers who were not native to the place would have to get out of the city. The town crier announced that in the future any of them who were found in the place would be punished with the whip. And so four days later, when the law went into effect, I saw a long line of paupers being whipped through the main streets. Which gave me such a fright that I never dared to risk begging after that.

Anybody with any imagination can envisage the resulting abstinence of my household, and the gloom and silence of the inhabitants. They were such that it was not unheard-of for two or three days to go by without our having a single bite to eat or a single word to say to each other. It was some women next door to us, cotton-spinners and bonnet-makers, with whom I'd struck up a neighborly acquaintance, who saved my life. Out of the miserable pittance which they earned they would give me a little something which made it possible for me to get by.

I wasn't as sorry for myself as I was for my poor master, who had not had a blessed bite of food for a week. In the house, anyway, neither of us ate at all, and I don't know where he was or what he ate when he was out. And to see him coming down the street at noon, drawn up to his full height, and leaner than a thoroughbred greyhound! And for the sake of that wretched commodity which he called his honor he would take a straw—and there weren't too many of them in the house, either—and go out the door picking his teeth, which had nothing in them to pick, and still grumbling about how it was an unlucky place to live, saying:

"It's sad to behold what this ill-fated dwelling is accomplishing. Just look at it: it's so dismal and dark and gloomy. We'll have nothing but trouble as long as we're there. I'll be overjoyed when the month is up, so that we can leave."

Well, one day while we were in this distressed, famished and dire condition, by some stroke of luck or other which I've never been very clear about, a *real* found its way into my master's miserable keeping. He brought it back to the house, as exuberant as though he had got hold of the treasures of Venice, and with an expression of the utmost gaiety and pleasure he handed it to me, saying:

"Here you are, Lazaro. God is becoming open-handed. Go down to the market and buy bread and wine and meat. Let's do it up proud! And what's more, you'll be glad to hear that I've rented another house and so we won't be staying on in this ill-starred building a day after the month is up. Damn the place anyway, and whoever put the first tile on the roof, for my troubles date from the moment I set foot inside the door. I swear by Our Lord that in the whole time I've lived in it I haven't swallowed one drop of wine nor eaten one bite of meat, and I haven't had a bit of rest, what with the looks of the place and its darkness and its gloom! Get along, hurry up, and today we'll eat like counts!"

I took my *real* and the jug and started up the street as fast as I could go, heading for the market. I was happy; I was overjoyed. But what was the use, for my miserable destiny has decreed that I am never to have any pleasure without some trouble coming with it. And that's how it turned out. Because as I was on my way up the street, already turning over in my mind how I could spend the money to the best advantage, and giving thanks to God for having seen to it that my master got some money, I had the bad luck to run right into a funeral coming down the street, with a lot of priests and people carrying a body along on a litter.

I flattened myself against the wall to get out of their way, and as the body went past there was a woman following just behind the litter, who I suppose must have been the wife of the dead man. She was in deep mourning, and there were a lot of other women with her. And as she went along she was sobbing out loud and saying:

"My husband and my lord, where are they taking you? To the sad and gloomy house, to the dark and dreary house, to the house where they neither eat nor drink!"

When I heard that it was as though the sky had fallen. I said:

"Oh misery! They're taking this dead man to my house!"

I turned back and, threading my way through all those people, I headed down the street again toward my house as fast as I could run. Once inside, I slammed the door shut behind me and implored my master to aid and protect me, clinging to him and coaxing him to come to my help and to defend the doorway. He was somewhat put about. And he imagined that I was referring to something else, and said to me:

"What's this? What's all the shouting about? What's the matter with you? Why were you in such a rage to shut the door?"

"Oh sir," I said, "come and help, for they're bringing a dead man here!"

"How's that?" he said.

"I ran across him up the street, and his wife was coming along saying to him: 'My husband and my lord, where are they taking you? To the dark and dreary house, to the sad and gloomy house, to the house where they neither eat nor drink.' They're bringing him here, sir."

And honestly, when my master heard that, although there was nothing particularly amusing about it, he laughed so hard that for a long time he couldn't say anything. In the meantime I had put the bar across the door and had my shoulder against it to make it even harder to open. The people went by with their dead man, but I was still afraid that they were going to put him in our house. My master may not have eaten his fill but he laughed his fill anyway, and when he'd finished he said to me:

"It's quite true, Lazaro. Taking the widow at her word, it's no wonder you came to that conclusion. But since God has ordained otherwise and they've gone past, open the door, open it and go get us something to eat."

"Just let them get around the corner at the end of the street, sir," I said.

Finally my master came to the street door and opened it, giving me the reassurance which I needed after the way I'd been frightened and upset, and I started out again. But even though we ate well that day I didn't get a damned bit of pleasure out of it. And it was three days before the color came back into my face. And my master went on finding it terribly funny, whenever he remembered what I'd thought, that time.

This was the sort of life which I led with my third master, the poor squire, for several days, and the whole time I was filled with curiosity about why he had come to that part of the country and why he was staying there. Because I'd known he was from somewhere else since my first day in his service. It was obvious from the fact that he knew so few of the local inhabitants and had so little to do with them.

Finally I got my wish and found out what I wanted to know. For one day when we had eaten fairly well and he was in a good humor, he told me about himself. He said he was from Old Castille, and that he'd left those parts rather than take his hat off to a knight who lived near him.

"Sir," I said, "if he was what you say he was and was of a higher station than you, weren't you wrong not to take your hat off first, since you say he took his off too?"

"He's what I say he is, and his station is superior to mine, and he did take his hat off to me, but when you think of all the times I took mine off first it would have been the least he could have done to have taken the initiative and got his off first once in a while."

"Sir," I said, "it seems to me that I wouldn't have looked at it that way when I was dealing with my superiors in rank and wealth."

"You're only a boy," he answered, "and you have no feelings for affairs of honor, which nowadays constitutes the man of breeding's only treasure. For I'd have you know that I'm a squire, but I swear to God that if I run across the Count in the street and

203

he doesn't take his hat off to me, and right off too, the next time
I see him coming I'll be careful to step aside into a house, as
though I had business there, or to go down another street, if I
can find one before he gets to me, rather than take my hat off to
him. Because a gentleman is obliged to nobody except God and
the King, and since he is a man of breeding it would be improper
for him to let his self-esteem suffer in the smallest detail. I remember one day in my own part of the country I put a tradesman
in his place and very nearly laid hands on him because every time
he met me he said to me, 'God keep Your Excellency.' 'As for
you, you base, miserable person,' I said to him, 'what's the matter
with your manners? Saying "God keep you" to me as though I
were just anybody.' After that, and to this day, he's taken off his
hat and addressed me properly."

"Isn't it alright," I asked him, "for one man to say 'God keep
you' to another, when he meets him?"

"What a damned fool notion!" he said. "You can address the
ignorant that way, but when it comes to men of higher birth, like
me, nothing less than 'I kiss Your Excellency's hands' is acceptable. Or at the very least, 'I kiss your hands, sir,' but that's only
if it's another gentleman who's addressing me. And that's why
when that boor at home tried to impose on me with his common
'keep you' I wouldn't put up with any more of it. And I wouldn't
then, and I won't now or in the future put up with any man from
the King down saying 'God keep you' to me."

"Sinner that I am," I said, "that's why God doesn't put Himself
out to keep you, because you won't let anybody ask Him to."

"Furthermore," he said, "I'm not so poor but that, in my own
part of the country I have lands and dwellings which, if they
were put into repair and well cultivated (they're sixteen leagues
from Valladolid, where I was born on a street that runs up the
hill) would be worth upwards of sixty times a thousand pennies—
to give you an idea of how extensive they are and how splendid
they might be made. And I have a dovecote which, if it weren't
falling down, as it is at the moment, would yield me better than
two hundred pigeons a year. And other things besides, which I
won't mention. And I left them all because my honor was at
stake. And I came to this city in the expectation of finding a good
position, but things have not turned out as I thought they would.
I've found plenty of canons and churchmen, but they're people
with such a limited point of view that nothing in the world would
get them to alter their ways. And there are the gentry of middling
importance who solicit my services, but it's gruelling working for

them because you have to play jack to their king, otherwise they give you their blessing and show you the door. And usually you have a long wait between one payment and the next, and as often as not you're lucky if you get your keep. And when they want to repair their conscience a bit and give you something in return for your exertions, you're paid off, in their dressing-room, with a sweaty doublet or a threadbare cloak or coat. Even if a man becomes a member of a nobleman's household, he needn't think his troubles are over. Do you think I'm not clever enough to serve one of them, by any chance, and to his complete satisfaction? By God, if I were to encounter one of them I'm sure I could become a great favorite with him, and have a thousand services to do for him, because I could lie to him as well as the next man, and afford him prodigies of delight. I'd laugh uproariously at all his witticisms and antics, even though they weren't the best in the world. I'd never tell him anything unpleasant, however much it might be to his advantage. I would be extremely solicitous of his person, both in word and deed, but I wouldn't kill myself being over-meticulous about things which he wasn't going to see. And I'd scold his servants where he was sure to hear me, so that he'd think I took endless pains over everything that had to do with him. But if he scolded one of them I'd slip in a few barbs to make him angry, while appearing to take the servant's part. I'd say nice things about everything that he liked, but on the other hand I'd be malicious, and a mocker, and a trouble-maker, both among members of the household and among outsiders. And I'd find ways of picking up bits of gossip to tell him, and develop a whole array of other talents of that sort, which are all the rage nowadays in palaces and are highly esteemed by the lords and masters there. Who have no wish to see men of virtue in their houses: they have an aversion to them, they look down on them, they call them fools and say that they're hopeless at practical affairs and are not men whom their masters can rely on. And with masters like that there are clever individuals nowadays practicing all the arts I've mentioned, and so could I, only I haven't had the luck to find one.

And my master went on in this way, bemoaning his hard lot and giving me a full account of what a gifted person he was.

Well, while we were still on this subject a man and an old woman came in at the door. The man wanted the rent for the house and the old woman the rent for the bed. They figured out what it all came to, and my master owed them more for two months than he could have got together in a whole year. I think it was twelve or thirteen *reales*. And he spoke very nicely to them and said he would just go down to the market to change a doubloon, and that they should come back in the afternoon. But he never showed up again.

So they came back in the afternoon, but too late. I told them that he hadn't returned. Night came, but he didn't, and I was afraid to stay in that house all by myself, and I went over to the neighbors and told them the whole story and slept there.

In the morning the creditors came back and came to the house where I was and inquired about the man next door, and the woman answered:

"Here's his servant, and the key to the door."

They asked me about him and I told them I didn't know where he was and that he hadn't been back since he went out to change the money and that in my opinion he'd given them the slip, and me along with them.

When they heard me say that they went for a constable and a notary, and brought them back along, and took the key and called me and several witnesses, and opened the door and went in to distrain upon my master's property until such time as his debt was paid. They went all over the house and found it empty, just as I've described it, and they said to me:

"Where are your master's possessions—his coffers and tapestries and valuables?"

"I don't know anything about that," I said.

They said, "He obviously carried them out last night and took them somewhere else. Constable, arrest that boy. He knows where they are."

Whereupon the constable came and took me by the collar of my coat and said:

"Boy, you're under arrest unless you tell us where your master's property is."

I'd never found myself in such a spot before—for though I'd been taken by the collar times without number, it had been done with a lighter touch, by the blind man, so that I could lead him. And I was terrified and started to cry, and promised to tell them anything they asked.

"Good," they said. "Now tell us everything you know, and don't be afraid."

The notary sat down on a stone bench to write the inventory, and asked me what the property consisted of.

"Sirs," I said, "according to what he told me, my master's

property consists of a fine estate, with houses on it, and a dovecote which is falling down."

"Good," they said. "However little they may be worth, they'll fetch enough to pay off the debt. In what part of the city is this property?" they asked me.

"In his own land," I answered.

"By God, what a business!" they said. "And where is his own land?"

"He said he came from Old Castille," I said.

The constable and the notary had a good laugh, and said:

"This account's good enough to cover your debt even if it came to more than it does."

The neighbors who were present said:

"Gentlemen, this child is innocent, and he's only been with the squire a few days and doesn't know any more about him than Your Worships do. For that matter the poor little sinner used to come over to our house a good bit of the time, and we'd give him something to eat when we could, out of holy charity, and then at night he'd come back over to the squire's to sleep."

They realized that I was innocent, and they let me go. And the constable and the notary asked the man and the woman for their fees. Which led to a terrible argument and racket. Because the man and the woman held that they weren't obliged to pay since there wasn't any property there to distrain on, and the others said that they'd left other business—and more profitable business too—in order to come and attend to this.

Finally, after they'd done a lot of shouting, the constable's deputy picked up the old woman's old mattress—and he didn't sag under the weight. And off they went, shouting at each other. I don't know how it ended. I suppose that disreputable mattress must have been made to pay for everything. Which would have served it right, for when it should have been retired and resting from its past labors, it was still going the rounds, hiring itself out.

And that was the way my poor third master left me, just as I've said, and it made me realize just how unfavorably inclined the fates were, where I was concerned. For they'd arrayed circumstances against me as thoroughly as they could, and had turned things so completely upside-down, in my case, that whereas it's the usual thing for servants to leave their masters, with me it turned out otherwise, and it was my master who left me and ran away.

How Lazaro Entered the Service of a Friar of the Order of Mercy, and What Happened to Him with that Master

I had to look for a fourth master. This one was a friar of the Order of Mercy, whom the women next door put me in touch with. They addressed him as one of the family. He was dead set against singing in choirs and eating in monasteries, but he had a passion for roaming around, and was extremely fond of secular affairs and making visits. To such a degree that I'm sure he wore out more shoes than all the rest of the monastery put together. He gave me the first shoes which I ever wore out in my life: they didn't last me a week. I couldn't have kept up with him much longer anyway. And because of this and a number of other little things which I won't mention, I left him.

How Lazaro Entered the Service of a Seller of Indulgences, and What Happened with that Master

The fifth one whom my fates led me to was a seller of indulgences. He was the most unscrupulous, shameless, and accomplished dealer in these articles that I ever saw or hope to see, or that I should think anybody else ever saw. For he had his own ways and means, and very ingenious tricks, and he kept working out new ones.

When he went into a place where he was going to peddle the pope's indulgences, the first thing he'd do was to make little presents to the priests. Nothing of any great value or importance: a head of Murcian lettuce, or a couple of limes or oranges when they were in season, or a peach or two, or one of those pears that are green even after they're ripe. That way he'd get them on his side, so that they were kindly disposed to his business, and they'd call out their parishioners to buy the pope's indulgences.

When the clerics thanked him he could get an idea of how learned they were. If they said they understood Latin he never spoke a word of it for fear he might make a mistake. Instead he would make use of an elegant and well-turned Spanish, and he was very smooth in that. And if he saw that the clerics in question were of that category of reverend gentlemen who acquire holy orders with money rather than with learning, he would carry on like Saint Thomas Aquinas and talk to them for two hours in Latin. At least it seemed that long even if it wasn't.

When the faithful were not eager to buy the indulgences he tried to force them to whether they wanted to or not. With this in view he could make a terrible nuisance of himself in a village. On other occasions he'd resort to the most ingenious tricks. It would take too long to describe all the things I saw him get up

209

to, so I'll tell about one particularly sly and artful dodge, which will give a good idea of how clever he was.

He'd been preaching for two or three days in a place in the Sagra de Toledo district, going through all his usual tactics, and they hadn't bought a single indulgence, and it didn't look to me as though they meant to buy any. He damned himself up and down in a fury, and thought it over, and made up his mind to call the whole place out, the next day, and unload his pardons on them.

And that night after supper he and the constable started gambling to see who should pay for the meal. And out of that a quarrel developed and there were some hard words. He called the constable a thief, and the constable said he was a cheat. At this point my master, the pope's representative, picked up a spear which was in the doorway near where they'd been gambling, and the constable took hold of the sword which he was wearing.

There was a lot of noise and shouting, to which we all contributed, and some of the guests from the inn, and some neighbors rushed to the scene and separated them. They were good and angry and they tried everything to get away from the people who were holding them, and kill each other. But the more noise there was, the more people came, until the house was full, and when the two of them saw that they weren't going to be able to use their weapons on each other, they used unsults instead. In the course of which the constable said that my master was not only a cheat but that his papal indulgences were forgeries.

Finally when the townspeople realized that they weren't going to be able to make peace between these two, they decided to take the constable somewhere else, away from the inn. Which further infuriated my master. Then the guests from the inn, and the neighbors, tried to calm him down, and in the end he went to bed, and so did all the rest of us.

In the morning my master went to the church and told them to ring the bell for the Mass at which he was to preach the sermon and sell off his pardons. The people congregated, muttering to each other about his indulgences as they came, saying that they were forgeries, and that it was the constable himself who had revealed this fact while the two of them were quarrelling. So that the ones who had been unenthusiastic about buying pardons before didn't want them now at any price.

My master, the pope's delegate, climbed up into the pulpit and started to preach and to work the people up not to remain any longer without the many benefits and indulgences which the papal certificate would confer upon them.

When he was at the height of all this, in through the door of the church came the constable, and when he'd said a prayer he stood up and began to speak very sagely, in a loud, deliberate voice. He said:

"Good people, let me have your attention for a moment. After that you can listen to whoever you please. I came here with this fraud who's preaching to you. He tricked me. He told me that if I would help him in this affair we would divide the proceeds. And now that I have realized the harm that this would do, both to my conscience and to your finances, I have repented of my agreement, and I declare to you unequivocally that the pardons which he is selling are forgeries, that you should not believe him nor buy any, that I have no part in them either directly or indirectly, and that I am resigning my office here and now, in token of which I throw my staff upon the ground. And if ever this man should come to be punished for his falsifications, I call upon you to bear me witness that I have nothing to do with him, that I am not helping him in any way, but that, quite the contrary, I am delivering you from his deceptions, and revealing his wickedness to you."

And that was the end of his speech. Several worthy gentlemen in the congregation wanted to pick up the constable and pitch him out of the church, to avoid a brawl. But my master held them back and requested them, on pain of excommunication, not to interfere with him, but to let him say anything he wanted to. And he didn't say anything either, while the constable was holding forth as I've recounted.

When he'd finished what he had to say, my master asked him if he didn't want to say something more, and urged him to say it. The constable said:

"There's a great deal more to be said on the subject of you and your tricks, but that's enough for the time being."

The pardoner got down on his knees in the pulpit, clasped his hands, raised his eyes to heaven, and said:

"Lord God, from whom nothing is hid, to whom all secrets are known, for whom nothing is impossible, Thou knowest the truth and how unjustly I have been insulted. As far as I personally am concerned, I forgive him, that Thou, Oh Lord, may forgive me. Do Thou pay no attention to this person who knows not what he does or says. But as for the injury which has been done to Thee, I implore Thee, and for the sake of justice I beg Thee, do not let that pass. Otherwise someone here present, who had perhaps considered purchasing this holy certificate of indulgence, might come to believe this man's falsehoods and not buy one after all. And on account of the grievous injury thereby done to his fellow men, Oh Lord, I beg of Thee, do not ignore this, but do Thou perform a miracle, here before our eyes, at this moment, and let it take the following form: if what he says is true, and I am purveying wickedness and falsehood, may this pulpit, with me in it, sink seven fathoms under the earth, where neither it nor I will ever be seen again. But if what I declare is the truth, and he has been led on by the promptings of the devil to rob and deprive those present of such inestimable benefits, and if what he says is false, then let him be punished, and let his villainy be apparent to all."

My reverend master had scarcely finished praying when the miserable constable fell off his bench and hit the floor with a thud you could hear all over the church, and started to bellow and foam at the mouth and screw his face up into weird expressions, flinging his feet and hands around and rolling back and forth over the floor.

The congregation set up such an uproar and shouting that nobody could hear anybody else. Some of them had quite a shock and were terrified.

Some of them said: "The Lord help and protect him."

And others: "Serves him right for bearing such false witness."

Finally a number of those present, and not without considerable trepidation, as I could see, went over to him and grabbed his arms—he was waving them around, whacking everybody near him with his fists. Others took him by the legs, and they hung on for dear life, because there never was a treacherous mule anywhere in the world who could give out kicks like those, for viciousness. So they held him for quite a while. And they had reason to: there were more than fifteen men on top of him and still they all had their hands full, he saw to that. And if they weren't careful he'd land them one on the nose.

The whole time this was going on, my master was up in the pulpit on his knees with his hands and eyes lifted heavenwards, and himself carried away into the essence of divinity to such a degree that all that stir and din in the church wasn't enough to fetch him back from his holy contemplation.

Some of the good people there went up to him and shouted until they woke him up, and they begged him to come and help the poor man, who was dying, and not to hold against him any of the things which he'd done, nor the terrible things he'd said, because he'd already received his punishment for those. But if there was anything at all that he could do which might alleviate the danger and torment which the man was going through, they begged him for the love of God to do it. For after all, the guilt of the guilty was now plain to them, as were his own truth and goodness, since, when he had made his request and called for vengeance, the Lord had not been backward with His punishments. My master the pardoner looked at them like somebody who is just waking up out of a sweet dream, and then he looked at the delinquent and at all the people who were standing around, and very slowly and deliberately he said to them:

"Good people, you should never plead for any man upon whom God has so manifestly manifested Himself. However, since He has commanded us not to return evil for evil, but to forgive the injuries which we are made to suffer, we can confidently implore His Majesty to do as He bids us do, and forgive this man who has trespassed against Him by placing an obstacle in the way of His Holy Faith. Let us all pray to Him."

And with these words he came down from the pulpit and there urged them to beseech Our Lord with all the devoutness they could bring to it, to pardon that sinner and restore him to his health and right mind, and to cast the devil out of him, if His Majesty, on account of the enormity of his sin, had allowed one to enter into him.

They all got down on their knees and they and the priests together began to chant a litany in a low voice before the altar. And my master came with the cross and the holy water, and when he had chanted over the constable he raised his hands to heaven and rolled up his eyes so that you couldn't see anything of them except a little bit of the white, and he started a prayer which was as long as it was devout and which made all the people cry the way they usually do during the sermons on the Passion, when the preachers and congregations are at their most devout. Since Our Lord, he said, surely did not desire the death of the sinner, but wanted him to live and repent having ever been led astray by the devil and seduced by death and sin, he begged Our Lord to pardon the sinner and grant him life and health so that he could repent and confess his sins.

When he'd finished praying he made them bring the indulgence and put it on the constable's head. And immediately that sinful constable began to get better, little by little, and return to his senses. And when he regained his wits he threw himself at the pardoner's feet and begged his forgiveness, and confessed that everything which he had said had been at the instigation of the devil, who had put the very words in his mouth. He'd behaved as he had, he said, in order to do harm to the pardoner and avenge his own anger—that was one reason. But the main one was that the devil was extremely upset about the good which might be done in that place by the sale of the indulgences.

My master forgave him and they were made friends again. And then there was such a rush to buy the pardons that there was scarcely a living soul in the place who was left without one— husband, wife, son, daughter, boy or girl.

The news of what had happened spread around through all the villages in the locality, and whenever they went to one of them they didn't even need to go to the church. The people would come right to the inn where they were staying, as though they were handing out pears for nothing. And so we did ten or twelve villages around there and my master sold ten or twelve thousand pardons without so much as having to preach a sermon.

When they tried this out the first time, I must admit to my shame that I was frightened by it like most of the others, and thought it was just what it appeared to be. But afterwards when I saw how my master and the constable laughed over the affair and made fun of it, I realized that it had all been worked out by my industrious and inventive master.

In another place, which for the sake of its honor I won't name, the following thing happened to us. My master preached a sermon or two and not a God-blessèd soul bought a pardon. He was sharp enough to see how it was going, and even when he told them that they could take a year to pay, it didn't do any good; they were so set against buying pardons that he was simply wasting his efforts. So he had them ring the bells for our farewell service, and when he'd finished his sermon and said good-bye to them from the pulpit, and was about to climb down, he called the clerk and me (I was weighed down with knapsacks) and he asked us to step up onto the first step. And he took all the pardons which the constable had in his hands, and he piled up at his feet the one that were in the knapsacks. Then he returned to his place in the pulpit, with a beaming expression on his face, and started tossing the indulgences out into the congregation, ten and twenty at a time, on all sides, saying:

"My brethren, take the grace which God sends you! Take it into your houses and be not sorrowful, for it is a most holy work we are engaged in—redeeming the Christians who are in captivity in the lands of the Moors. Help them with your alms and with five paternosters and five ave-marias, to the end that they may not deny our holy faith and may be brought forth out of captivity. And your money will also benefit your parents and brothers and sisters and other relatives in Purgatory, as you can see on this holy indulgence."

When the villagers saw him tossing them from the pulpit as though he were giving away something for nothing, and as though they were raining from the hand of God, they scrambled for them. They got copies for the babies in their cradles and for all the dead people in their families, and for all their children and the servants in their houses right down to the very least important of them, counting them on their fingers. The pace was so brisk that they virtually tore to shreds a ragged old jacket which I had on, and I assure Your Excellency that in just a little over an hour there wasn't a single indulgence left in the knapsacks and I had to go back to the inn and fetch some more.

When they'd taken all there were, my master, up in the pulpit, called to his own clerk and the clerk of the town council to get to their feet and find out the names of those who were going to benefit by this holy indulgence, and he told them to write them all down so that he'd have an accurate account of everybody who now had copies.

And so the next thing was that all the ones who'd taken copies were only too delighted to give their names, and also—all in the right order—the names of their children and their servants, and the dead people in their families.

When he had drawn up the list he explained to the justices of the peace that he had other places to get to, and he asked them in the name of charity to allow the clerk to authorize the list and keep a record of all those who were there, and according to the notary there were upwards of two thousand.

When all this was done he took his leave with a great deal of good will and affection, and with that we left the place. And even then, before we got away, the local curate and the magistrates came up to him to inquire whether the indulgence extended to the creatures who were as yet in their mothers' wombs.

He told them that according to the literature which he had studied on the subject, it did not. He said that they should go and consult with older scholars than himself, and that this was merely his own opinion on this particular subject.

And so we left and went on our way, all of us delighted with the success of our business there. My master said to the constable and the clerk:

"What do you think of these peasants who simply say we're old Christians and expect that to save them, without their performing any acts of charity or handing over any of their worldly goods? I swear by the life of Pascasio Gomez the lawyer, I'd be amazed if more than ten souls were set free on *their* account."

So we went on to another place, outside Toledo on the way to La Mancha, as they say, where we stumbled on some who were a bit more obstinate about buying pardons. My master and all the rest of us gave of our best in two fairs in the locality and at the end of it we had not sold thirty of the indulgences.

My master realized that perdition was upon us, that we were on the way to ruin, and he was clever enough to think up a trick for unloading the pardons. He said high mass that day and when the sermon was over and he had gone back to the altar he took a cross which he had with him—it was a little over a hand's-breadth in size—and without anybody noticing, he slipped it onto the lighted brazier which was up on top of the altar where it had been put for him to warm his hands at, because it was very cold, and then he hid the whole thing in back of the missal. And there he managed to suspend the cross over the flame, without letting on about it, and when he had finished mass and pronounced the benediction he took a handkerchief and wrapped it carefully around the cross, and then picked it up in his right hand and the pardon in the other and thus equipped he descended to the bottom step of the altar, where he invited them to come and kiss the cross. He beckoned them to come and worship the cross. And the magistrates came first, and the elders of the place, one by one, in the usual way. The first of them was an old magistrate and when he got up to the altar my master told him to kiss the cross very lightly, but even so he burned his kisser and jumped back in a hurry. When my master saw that, he said:

"Soft! Hush, my lord justice! A miracle!"

And seven or eight others did the same thing and he said to all of them:

"Soft, my lords! A miracle!"

When he saw that there were enough burnt kissers to serve as witnesses of the miracle, he refused to let any more kiss the cross. He stepped down to the foot of the altar and there he said wonderful things to them, telling them that on account of their lack of charity God had permitted this miracle in their midst, and that this cross would be taken up to the cathedral of the bishopric, and that it was on account of the lack of charity in their town that the cross had burned.

They were in such a rush to get the pardon that two clerks and all the priests and sacristans in the place weren't enough to keep up with the names. I'm convinced that they bought more than three thousand of the pardons, as I've told your worship.

Later, when he was on the point of leaving, he proceeded to take up the blessèd cross with great reverence, which it deserved after all, and as he did so he mentioned that he was going to have it encased in gold, which it also deserved.

But the municipal council and the priests of the town implored him to leave the holy cross with them, in memory of the miracle which had taken place there. He wouldn't hear of such a thing, but then in the end there were so many of them begging him for it that he did leave it with them. And in its place they gave him another old cross which they had there; it was ancient, made of silver, and it weighed as much as two or three pounds, according to them.

And so we went away happy at the good bargain we'd made and the good business we'd done there. Nobody had noticed anything of the above except me. Because I'd climbed up onto the altar to see whether there was anything left in the receptacles, and to put it in a safe place, as I was in the habit of doing. And when he saw me there he put his finger on his mouth to tell me to keep still. And so I did, because he took good care of me, although when I'd seen the miracle I was burning to tell somebody. But I was too frightened of my clever master to let on to anybody, and I never said a word. I swore to him that I'd never tell on him about the miracle, and I never have until now.

And though I was only a boy, I thought it was a very funny routine, and I said to myself:

"What a lot of tricks of this kind these sharks must play on innocent people!"

Altogether I spent four months with this fifth master, and during that time too I suffered plenty of hardships, although he did give me enough to eat—at the expense of the priests and other clergy in the towns where he went to preach.

How Lazaro was Employed by a Chaplain, and What Happened to Him There

After that I was employed by a master tambourine painter, to grind his colors, and there too I had my troubles.

By that time I was a good-sized boy, and one day when I went into the cathedral a chaplain took me into his employment. He put me in charge of a donkey and four water jars and a whip, and I set out around the city, selling water. This was my first step upwards toward a decent way of life, for I ate regularly. Every day I turned over to my master thirty *maravedis* profit. Everything I earned on Saturdays I could keep for myself, and everything above thirty *maravedis* which I earned on week days.

I did so well at this trade that at the end of the four years which I spent at it, by carefully putting aside my money I'd saved up enough to outfit myself decently in a suit of second-hand clothes. I bought an old fustian doublet and a threadbare coat with braid on the sleeves and collar, and a cloak which at one time had had a thick nap, and a sword—one of the first ones Cuellar ever made. Once I was respectably dressed I told my master to take back his donkey because I didn't want to follow that trade any more.

How Lazaro was Employed by a Constable, and What Happened to Him with that Master

After I left the chaplain I took a position with a constable, as his bailiff. But I scarcely stayed with him any time at all, because it struck me as a dangerous calling. Especially one night, when several fugitives from justice chased my master and me with stones and clubs. And they were extremely rough with my master, who stayed behind. As for me, they never caught up with me. After that I called off our arrangement.

And as I was trying to think of some employment at which I could earn my living, which would provide me with a bit of security and something toward my old age, it pleased God to enlighten me and set me going on a profitable road. And with the help which I got from friends and superiors, all the hardships and troubles which I had endured up until then were made up for by my achieving my ambition. Which was a post in the government. For I had noticed that nobody really thrives except those who have positions of that nature.

In which post I have continued to this day, in the service of God and Your Excellency. My function is to cry up the wines which are to be sold in this city, and to announce auctions and lost articles, and to go along beside those who are being prosecuted for the sake of justice, and call out what crimes they committed: in good plain terms, I'm a town crier.

In the performance of this office, one day when we were hanging a petty thief from Toledo, who was wearing a good quality hempen rope, this detail caught my attention, and my mind went back to what my blind master had said in Escalona, and I was sorry to have made him such a graceless return for all that he'd taught me. For next to God himself, it had been he who'd given me most of the qualifications which made it possible for me to attain my present position.

I've made out so well in it, and used my post to such good effect, that virtually everything there is in that line of business goes through my hands now. So that all over the city, if anybody has wine to sell, or anything else, unless Lazaro de Tormes attends to it they can make up their minds that it won't show any profit to speak of.

At this point my lord the Archpriest of San Salvador, a friend and servant of Your Excellency's, took notice of me as a result of my crying his wines for him, and in view of my ability and prosperity, formed a project to marry me to a girl in his service. And since I realized that I stood to gain a great deal from such a personage, I agreed. And so I married her, and I have not yet come to regret it.

Because not only is she herself a good girl, and hard-working and accommodating, but my lord the Archpriest has helped me and favored me in all sorts of ways. And he gives her a bit of wheat now and then—in the course of a year it must add up to four or five bushels. And at Easter there's meat, and from time to time there are a couple of loaves of holy bread, and we always get his old hose when he's finished with them. And he's rented me a little house next to his, and nearly every Sunday and holiday we eat in his house.

But there never was a shortage of evil tongues, and there never will be, and they never give us a rest, saying that I don't know— or that I do know—what goes on when my wife goes to make his bed and cook his meals. And may God treat them better than they treat the truth.

Though all this time I've felt just a little bit suspicious, and there've been some bad supper times when I've waited for her at night until lauds and even later, and I've been reminded of what my master the blind man said to me in Escalona, with his hand on the horn. Though to tell the truth I always think that the devil brings that back to mind in order to sow discord between man and wife, and he gets nowhere that way.

Because she's a woman who doesn't care for that kind of carrying on, and furthermore my lord the Archpriest has made me a promise and I'm counting on him to fulfil it. One day he spoke to me at some length, in her presence, and he said to me:

"Lazaro de Tormes, nobody who pays attention to malicious gossip will ever get anywhere. I mention this because it would not surprise me at all if somebody, seeing your wife come and go in my house . . . Her being here redounds to her own honor and yours, too, I can assure you of that. Consequently, you'd do well to ignore anything which they're likely to say, except what concerns you, by which I mean your own advantage."

"Sir," I said, "I have made up my mind to cleave unto the good. To be honest, some of my friends have said something of the sort to me, and for that matter have sworn three times and upwards that she'd had three children before she married me, speaking with all due reverence for Your Worship, and with her there to hear me."

Whereupon my wife began to swear such oaths that I thought the house would be swallowed up with us inside it. And then she started to cry and to curse the man who'd married her to me. She made such a fuss that I'd rather have died than to have said what I did. But I took one side of her and my lord the other and between us we wheedled and promised her until she stopped crying. I had to swear never again, as long as I lived, to so much as refer to anything of that nature, and to declare that I was quite content that she should come and go, day or night, since I was entirely convinced of her virtue. So all three of us were happy.

And to this day nobody's heard us mention the subject. Indeed, if I feel that anybody is likely to say something about it, I cut him short and say:

"Look, if you're a friend of mine don't say things to me which are bound to upset me, because I don't think that's the part of a friend. Especially if they will only lead to trouble with my wife. For she's the one thing which I cherish most in this world, and I love her more than myself. And in her God has showered me with blessings, far more than I deserve. For I'll swear by the Consecrated Host that she's as virtuous as any woman living within the gates of Toledo, and if any man says otherwise, I'm his enemy to the death."

So they don't say anything about it, and there's peace in the house.

All this took place in the same year that our victorious emperor entered this renowned city of Toledo and held his court here, as Your Excellency no doubt has heard. At which time I had entered into my prosperity and had attained the summit of all good fortune.

As to what happens to me from now on, I shall keep Your Excellency informed.

W.S. Merwin

W.S. Merwin was born in New York City in 1927 and grew up in Union City, New Jersey, and in Scranton, Pennsylvania. From 1949 to 1951 he worked as a tutor in France, Portugal, and Majorca. After that, for several years he made the greater part of his living by translating from French, Spanish, Latin and Portuguese. Since 1954 several fellowships have been of great assistance. In addition to poetry, he has written articles, chiefly for *The Nation*, and radio scripts for the BBC. He has lived in Spain, England, France, Mexico and Hawaii, as well as New York City. His books of poetry are *A Mask for Janus* (1952), *The Dancing Bears* (1954), *Green with Beasts* (1956), *The Drunk in the Furnace* (1960), *The Moving Target* (1963), *The Lice* (1967), *The Carrier of Ladders* (1970), for which he was awarded the Pulitzer Prize, *Writings to an Unfinished Accompaniment* (1973), *The Compass Flower* (1977), and *Opening the Hand* (1983). His translations include *The Poem of the Cid* (1959), *Spanish Ballads* (1960), *The Satires of Persius* (1961), *Lazarillo de Tormes* (1962), *The Song of Roland* (1963), *Selected Translations 1948-1968* (1968), for which he won the P.E.N. Translation Prize for 1968, *Transparence of the World*, a translation of his selection of poems by Jean Follain (1969), *Osip Mandelstam, Selected Poems* (with Clarence Brown) (1974), *Selected Translations, 1968-1978* (1979), *From the Spanish Morning* (1985), and *Four French Plays* (1985). He has also published three books of prose, *The Miner's Pale Children* (1970), *Houses and Travellers* (1977) and *Unframed Originals* (1982). In 1974 he was awarded The Fellowship of the Academy of American Poets. In 1979 he was awarded the Bollingen Prize for Poetry.